PUB V

DAVID HANCOCK

Ensign

First published in 1993 by
Ensign Publications
2 Redcar Street,
Southampton SO1 5LL.

a b c d

Publisher David Graves.
Designed by Precinct Press.
Cover by Design Laboratory.
Cover photo. by Terry Heathcote.
Text photos. by Bonita Toms.
Maps by Jack Street.
Printed by Short Run Press, Exeter.

ISBN 185455 093 4

Walk · CONTENTS · Page

· INTRODUCTION ·

The magnificent landscape that surrounds the majestic city of Salisbury is perfect walking country. It is a land dominated to the north by the broad expanse of Salisbury Plain, on which rise five rivers that meander south and east, etching delightful valleys through the chalk downland hills to converge on Salisbury.

Undulating chalk country extends north-east from Salisbury into some truly unspoilt areas of North Hampshire, in particular the idyllic Test Valley and the 'Hampshire Highlands' that surround the attractive market town of Andover.

This selection of carefully crafted, circular walks explore the web of footpaths and bridleways that criss-cross this land of panoramic views and sheltered scenic valleys. Many are ancient drove-ways linking historic towns and villages and exploring archaeological sites and monuments. All the walks are between 4 and 8 miles and in addition to the comprehensive route descriptions, each ramble is accompanied by a precise sketch map, the approximate length of walk and minimum time they should take to complete and a special feature, unique to this series, detailing the historical background of places of interest along the route and of the villages and hamlets in the surrounding area.

A welcoming sight after a three-hour stroll that has stimulated a healthy appetite and a parched throat is an unspoilt, traditional country pub. Each walk starts and finishes from just such a pub and the book includes detailed information concerning opening times, bar and restaurant food choices and serving times, the range of real ales and facilities for children.

Most landlords are happy to allow people who have used their pub for eating or drinking to use their car park while they complete one of these walks. However we strongly recommend that you do ask the pub's permission before setting off for your ramble. Concise directions are supplied in the 'How to get there' section for car drivers to locate the pub in the first place and for public transport users.

Most of the routes are on country paths which can be extremely muddy, especially so after wet weather, so stout footwear is advisable. Remember to carry a light waterproof garment and a walking stick can be useful for navigating some of the less-used tracks through overgrown woodland. Always observe the country code — fasten all gates behind you, keep dogs under proper control and always on a lead when there are livestock around, do not damage property, keep to the public rights of way, do not dig up wild plants and leave nothing behind you but your footprints. Happy pub walking!

DAVID HANCOCK
October 1993

Exploring Wardour Park footpaths from Ansty

WALK 1
Allow 4 hours
6 miles
Walk begins page 7

Background to the Walk

Ansty is a scattered community of predominantly thatched houses strung out along the little brook of Ansty Water, which swells the River Nadder at nearby Tisbury.

The history of the village can be traced far back in time. During the Saxon period Ansty bordered a rough track which led up through the valley to join the ancient highway, on the crest of the chalk downs, which linked Salisbury and Shaftesbury long before the turnpike at the base of the hill was made. The village derives its name from the Saxon word 'Anestige', meaning 'the way up'. The village later became part of the Royal Forest of Selwood and it is said that King Alfred, who founded a monastic community in Shaftesbury, used to hunt near Ansty. Successive kings of Wessex came to the forests surrounding the village to enjoy the fruits of the rich hunting ground and fertile farmland.

Ansty's importance grew through its royal connections. Domesday records that the village was bound to provide one knight for the King's service, then in 1211, during the reign of King John, the Manor of Ansty title deeds were given the Knights Hospitaller of the Order of St. John of Jerusalem. This was in gratitude for the Knights' services in the Crusades and also to ensure the sacraments would be available when the court of St. John was in residence in the neighbourhood.

A Commandery was formed and this small group built the church of St. James, which was completed in 1230, the large fishpond and a hospice which tended pilgrims on their way to the Abbey at Shaftesbury. The

Maps
Landranger 1:50,000
Sheet 184
Pathfinder 1:25,000
Sheet ST 82/92
Map Reference of Start/
Finish ST957265

How to get there
Ansty lies just off A30, approximately 12 miles west of Salisbury. From Salisbury town centre follow signs for The West A30, A303 towards Wilton and Warminster on the A36. At the roundabout at Wilton turn left, pass through the village keeping straight on over the traffic lights to follow A30 for 10 miles, through Barford and Fovant. Ansty is signposted right just beyond Swallowcliffe. From Andover take A3057 Romsey road south, then join A303 and head west before leaving at the first junction to follow A343 for Salisbury. Merge with A30 and proceed into Salisbury. At the first main roundabout take fourth exit and follow signs for Warminster and The West.

Pub facilities
Maypole Inn, Ansty
This attractive brick and flint village inn, built in about 1825 as an ale house for the workers on the Wardour estate, was originally known as the Arundell Arms, after

the long-established owners of Wardour Castle. Appropriately renamed The Maypole Inn in 1973 as the 96 ft. maypole is just a stone's throw away. Tubs of flowers and picnic benches to the front make a peaceful spot to enjoy a drink and a warm welcome awaits walkers. The one bar is neatly arranged with two fires — one open — modern settles, a church pew, wheel-back chairs and darkwood tables laid out for diners. A collection of plates, village photographs and hunting prints adorn the walls. The bar opens from 1100-1430 (1200-1500 on Sunday) and 1830-2300 Tuesday to Saturday. The pub is closed Sunday evening and all day Monday. It is a free house serving two real ales — Wadworth 6X and Butcombe Bitter. Bar food extends from a hearty snack menu featuring ham, egg and chips, ploughmans, jacket potatoes and freshly cut sandwiches to more substantial dishes, such as seafood au gratin and mushroom crepe for starters, followed by grilled pork chop, half a roast chicken, seafood or ham platter, steaks, a range of fresh fish includes trout, plaice, cod — plus vegetarian nut roast Portuguese. Puddings include fruit pie, chocolate mousse and spotted dick and custard. Food is served from 1200-1400 and 1900-2130. Children over five are welcome in the dining area. Dogs are not allowed inside. Three letting bedrooms. Walkers may use the rear car park, if they ask permission first.

The attractive Maypole Inn at Ansty, built around 1825

building that now stands on the site of the hospice measures 110 feet by 30 feet and has been used as a wheelwright's and a workshop. Ansty Manor on the west side of the pond was probably the domestic building of the Commandery. This fine collection of buildings grouped around the pond is considered to be the finest example of a Commandery of the Order of St. John to have survived in England.

At the northern end of the pond is the Maypole Inn, which is named after the 96 foot-high maypole — claimed to be the highest in England — that stands in the lane nearby. The tradition of the maypole in Ansty is said to date from the time when the tenants of Wardour estate brought their children to be 'introduced' to each other. The annual Mayday celebrations are still a major event in the village. Every 25 years, when the maypole — a Douglas fir — needs to be replaced, the new pole must be put up between midnight and the following noon so that the road is not obstructed for more than twelve hours. It is a tradition that is maintained in order to keep the maypole in the village road.

The major part of our walk explores the secluded wooded parkland that surrounds the ruins of Old Wardour Castle, which is situated in a truly romantic and peaceful lakeside setting. It was built in 1393 by Lord Lovel and reconstructed in 1578 by Sir Matthew

Arundell. It was not built as a fortress in the familiar sense of the word 'castle', but as a tower house for comfort and lavish entertainment, at the same time equipped with some defensive provisions. There is no other castle like it in England, for it is hexagonal in shape and unlike many castles where the various rooms and chambers required by a great household were dispersed in towers and often in separate buildings, at Old Wardour everything is contained within one building.

During the Civil War in 1643 the castle had to be defended against a Commonwealth army. A garrison of only 50 soldiers and servants, along with Lady Arundell, conducted an heroic defence of Old Wardour, holding out for six days against 1300 of Cromwell's regulars. She surrendered only when offered honourable terms, which the Roundheads immediately broke, sacking the Castle and imprisoning Lady Arundell. Later her son besieged the Parliamentary garrison in turn and blew up his home rather than leave it in their hands. Lady Arundell is believed to have escaped by a secret passage to nearby Pyt House.

The Castle was never restored after the war, a smaller house being built to one side. In the early 18th century the ruins were surrounded by formal gardens, creating the flavour of a romantic ruin within a 'richly contrived' setting. Between 1769-76 New Wardour Castle was designed in a Palladian style by James Paine for the 8th Lord Arundell and built on a splendid site on the other side of the Park. It remained the seat of the Arundell family until 1944. It has since been a school, but at present it is being renovated by English Heritage and not open to the public.

Walk 1

Distance: *Allow at least four hours for this six mile walk, longer if you plan to visit the ruins of Old Wardour Castle.*

On leaving the inn turn left along the narrow hedged lane towards Ansty Coombe, passing Hillside Farmhouse. Gently rise uphill to a crossroads where a good view north, towards Tisbury and the Nadder Valley, can be enjoyed from the metal gate on your right. Keep ahead along this delightfully quiet lane, which was lined with the yellows of celendines and primroses on the fine spring day we walked this way. Your route keeps left at the next junction, then just beyond a thatched cottage, step over a tiny stream and immediately pass through an old wooden gate on your right. The grassy area in the vicinity of the gate was very wet and boggy, due to its position at the base of the hill, the recent rainfall and the proximity of the stream.

Two yellow arrows offer a choice of paths, our course follows the right-hand edge of the pasture uphill to a stile that precedes woodland. Tranquil unspoilt views begin to open up behind you across the scattered houses of Ansty. Climb the stile and shortly bear right along a wide grassy pathway that skirts the edge of Twelve Acre Copse and affords lovely views. Where this veers into the woodland to a junction of trackways, bear left, then left again to join a wide earth track that heads uphill into the thick predominantly coniferous woodland. Holly and laurel line your route, then where the woodland begins to thin, a carpet of bluebells will greet the eye if walking this path in May.

Proceed straight ahead on reaching a crossroads of tracks and emerge from the woodland to another earth trackway that cuts across your route. Keep ahead to follow a wide fenced bridleway. Away to your left, the chalk escarpment of the West Wiltshire Downs — Ansty Down and Whitesheet Hill — dominate the skyline, the latter rising to 900 feet. The ridge carries the ancient drove route that once linked Salisbury to Shaftesbury.

Your wide trackway bisects two large arable fields and leads you towards another area of coniferous woodland, known as Wardour Woods with sections called The Hanging and High Wood. This mature woodland covers a ridge of hills that surround Old Wardour Castle and its sheltered vale. Soon enter the wood, the track became extremely muddy, the result of recent rain and the passage of heavy tree cutting machinery, as we began to descend steeply through the wood. The track becomes walled on your left, then just beyond a fine stone archway the majestic ruin of Old Wardour Castle can be glimpsed through the trees to your left. Standing on a spur within the crescent of wooded high ground the Castle enjoys serene views westwards across its park and the Nadder Valley.

Eventually emerge out of the woods at the parking area and Castle entrance which lies to your left. The Castle is in the care of English Heritage and is open daily to the public at a small charge. Our walk passes the entrance and follows the old wall down towards the lake. On reaching a track turn left through the wooden gate, your path is waymarked to the 'Donheads'. The trackway passes between the Castle and its lake and allows the opportunity to savour the real splendour of the Castle's landscaped gardens and romantic lakeside setting.

Shortly, pass the Gothic Pavilion, then at Wardour House (private) bear right with the trackway which gradually climbs uphill around Cresswell Pond and away from the Castle. It is worth pausing regularly to enjoy the beautiful wood-land setting that Old Wardour Castle nestles within. The wide established track soon skirts woodland and affords peaceful rural vistas across the parkland to the vast Palladian mansion of New Wardour Castle, which was built in the 18th century. At a fork in the track, keep left, then at the end of the woodland where the track terminates, cross a stile beside a field entrance and proceed straight ahead along the right-hand edge of pasture. Gently descend towards some woodland and a pond. Climb a stile beside a field entrance (usually strung with barbed wire) and walk along a defined earth track or causeway between two ponds — Pale Park Pond and Heron Pond — to a stile beside a metal gate at the far end.

Beyond the stile bear half-right steeply uphill towards a gate that precedes woodland ahead. Climb the stile beside the gate, then in a little way bear left along a track to reach the main forest thoroughfare and turn right. The clearing of trees to your right has revealed a splendid rural scene across the Nadder Valley and New Wardour Castle. Remain on this track to a squeeze stile beside a wooden gate and leave the wood to join a gravel track that leads you to the left of a house. At the end of the gravel drive go through a walk through stile on your right and head downhill across pasture to a metal gate on the edge of woodland. Rolling

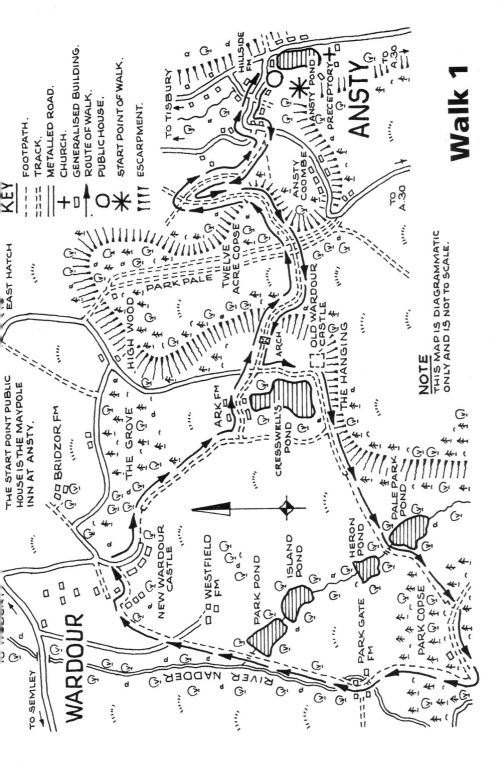

Walk 1

countryside and the Donhead villages can be viewed to your left. Descend through the wood on a narrow worn path, then soon bear left down a wide clearing at the woodland fringe towards Park Gate Farm visible in front of you. After passing a wildlife observation tower go through a walk through stile that flanks a field entrance, then proceed ahead along the right-hand edge of the field to the farm and turn right into the farmyard.

Your route keeps left across the yard, crosses the River Nadder and leaves the farm via a black-painted gate. Almost immediately go through the gate on your right and keep right-handed to a small brick bridge over the river. An unusual wooden footbridge on top of the bridge, obviously designed to keep animals out, leads you into a further meadow. Here you bear left along the hedge, your route heading north parallel to the river. A good stretch of level walking brings you to two stiles, beyond which you bear diagonally left across pasture, aiming for the left-hand side of the cottage ahead. Pass over a small footbridge, then head uphill to a stile in the fence beside the cottage. Cross the concrete drive to Westfield Farm and the stile beyond and head straight uphill, keeping to the left of the tree and walk towards the wood in front of you.

A walk through stile leads you onto an established path through the wood, its base a mass of wild garlic when we walked this way. Your path passes to the left of three houses, then bears right in front of the properties and veers left beside a brick outhouse, the defined path passing a conifer tree and crosses the grounds to New Wardour Castle which looms to your right. The sad state of the gardens and statues gave an air of faded grandeur to the place. Pass a water tap, drop down a couple of steps and keep ahead along a grass centred track, soon to turn right along the main driveway to the mansion. One of the side buildings was draped in scaffolding and plastic sheeting, indicating that the English Heritage was spending much time and money in renovating this vast building. Scruffy, run down classrooms tacked onto one side give clear evidence that this was once used as Cranborne Chase School.

The tarmac path leads you past the building and soon gives way to an unmetalled trackway. Shortly, where this track divides, keep left across a stile beside a metal gate and keep ahead on an established trackway through the parkland towards Old Wardour Castle. When you reach a metal gate, climb the metal stile alongside, then bear left onto a stony grass centred track and follow this to Ark Farm. Pass through the farm building complex and bear left along the main farm drive away from the farmhouse. This pitted tarmac drive soon leads you back to the car park to Old Wardour Castle. Keep left-handed through the car park to rejoin your outward route which heads uphill into the woodland that surrounds the Castle. From here the return route retraces your steps back to the Maypole Inn and your car.

Downland Ways from Ebbesbourne Wake

WALK 2
Allow 3 hours
5 miles
Walk begins page 13

Background to the Walk

This five mile ramble is one of three in and around the unspoilt Ebble Valley, this particular walk explores the upper reaches of the thirteen mile long stream. The River Ebble or Chalkebourne rises near Alvediston and flows eastwards towards Salisbury, merging with the River Avon just south of the city. The valley, unlike many that radiate from Salisbury, is thankfully free from the intrusions and noise that a main road brings to an area. A series of narrow lanes link the delightful villages that are strung along the river's length and to the north and south high chalk downs shelter the peaceful rural landscape.

The Ebble at Ebbesbourne Wake is in its infancy and generally is only in flow during the winter months when rainwater saturates the chalk. It really only becomes a stream when a larger chalk stream from Bowerchalke merges with the Ebble down the valley. The village name derives from the original Saxon personal name 'Ebbel' and the 'bourne' from the chalk stream — hence 'Ebble's Bourne'. A 'bourne' is an intermittent chalk stream which disappears underground in dry weather, only to reappear when wetter conditions prevail. The 'Wake' part of the name was added when a manor was granted in 1205 to Galfridas, otherwise Geoffrey de Wake. The village is one of my favourites west of Salisbury, for it nestles beneath the downs on a tiny lane, oblivious to 20th century hustle and bustle. A collection of neat thatched cottages are congregated around the 15th century church, which stands on the hill and close to the gem of a simple and unspoilt village inn — The Horseshoe.

Maps
Landranger 1:50,000
Sheet 184
Pathfinder 1:25,000
Sheet ST 82/92
Map Reference of Start/
Finish ST994241

How to get there
Ebbesbourne Wake lies 10 miles west of Salisbury. From the town centre head south and join A354 for Blandford Forum and Dorchester, after 2 miles turn right onto an unclassified lane in Coombe Bissett for Bishopstone. Follow the valley road for 8 miles via Broad Chalke to Ebbesbourne Wake. From Andover follow A3057 south for Stockbridge and Romsey, then head west along A303 for 1 mile before joining A343 signed to Salisbury. Merge with A30 and continue into the city, following 'through traffic' signs south to pick up A354 Blandford road. Wilts and Dorset service 29 between Salisbury and Shaftesbury via the Chalke Valley stops in Ebbesbourne Wake and Alvediston from Monday to Saturday. Wilts and Dorset/ Hampshire Bus services 7, 8, 9 and Hants. Bus services 76/ 76A link Andover with Salisbury as does the railway.

The Horseshoe, Ebbesbourne Wake

Pub facilities
Horseshoe,
Ebbesbourne Wake
Situated sideways on to the village lane, this mellow-brick 18th century inn is the epitome of a true homely village inn. What was formerly hatch door service has been converted into two simple and friendly bars. The main bar has a huge inglenook with real winter log fire, an assortment of rustic furniture and is festooned with an extensive collection of old tools and rural artifacts, which crowd the beams and walls. The other bar is tiny with a few tables and chairs and further farming memorabilia. It is very much a free house dispensing a good range of ales straight from the cask — Ringwood Best, Adnams Best, Wadworth 6X and a few winter guest brews. These as well as Thatchers farm cider can be sampled from 1100 (1200 Mondays)-1430 and 1830 (1900 Mondays)-2300 and during the usual Sunday hours. Bar food is very popular, especially the set Sunday lunch which is excellent value and served in the small dining room — booking essential. Simple, yet hearty snacks and meals can be ordered in the bar and may include freshly cut sandwiches, home-made soup, trout pate, ploughmans, steak and kidney pie served with a good vegetable selection, lemon sole with crab meat, chicken filled with prawns and lobster, pork with Stilton, chicken and mushroom pie and locally made faggots. Food is served from 1200-1400 and 1900-2130, the dining room only open in the evening and at Sunday lunchtime.

To the north high above the village is the great chalk mass of the West Wiltshire Downs and in particular Swallowcliffe Down and Whitesheet Hill. Along the length of the ridgeway runs an ancient hill-top route, known as the Salisbury Way and its importance in the earliest of days can be traced through the presence of earthworks, barrows, tumulli and a little way east, the Iron Age settlement of Chiselbury camp. In prehistoric times the ridge would have been much favoured by travellers for it offered an open and dry passage. During medieval times the Salisbury Way continued to be the main route linking Salisbury to the west, especially for pilgrims travelling to Wilton and Shaftesbury abbeys. In later years the route was used by horse-drawn coaches on route from London to Exeter, until improved road-making techniques in the 19th century made it possible for a new road to be built along the base of the downs in the Nadder Valley. The Salisbury Way is now a deserted grassy track used by local farmers and ramblers.

Further up the valley lies the tiny scattered village of Alvediston, or 'Ellofadistance' as it is called by the locals. Exactly where they are so far from is not certain, but it may refer to where the Ebble meets the Avon to the east or possibly to the long walk uphill from the village to the top of Swallowcliffe Down! The history of the village dates back to medieval times and one of the

Children are welcome in the top bar or the dining room if they are eating. A pretty terraced garden with flowers, trees and shrubs overlooks the Ebble Valley and the adjacent paddock has a Pot-Bellied pig, goats, cats and a donkey to keep the children amused on fine days. The inn has three letting bedrooms.

oldest families in England, the Gawens, who lived at the magnificent Norrington Manor and are thought by some to be descended from the legendary knight Sir Gawain, of King Arthur's Round Table fame. It is thought the original Manor was built in the time of Richard II and that the Gawens completed the present building after 1377. Much of the 14th century building still stands with some 17th century additions. It lies in the hills and is passed on our walk.

Memorials to the Gawen family and the Wyndham family who succeeded them at Norrington can be seen in the delightful little church of St. Mary, which lies to the north of the village overlooking the meadows. The original 13th century church was rebuilt in 1866 by T. H. Wyatt and the earliest remaining architectural features are 17th century, including the Perpendicular tower. In the south transept of the church is a tomb of a knight in armour, this is thought to be that of John Gawen and dates from the late 14th century. Pride of place at the front of the churchyard is the tomb of Sir Anthony Eden, Earl of Avon and Prime Minister between 1955 and 1957 who died in 1977. He lived in the brick-built 18th century Manor House, which is located close to the church.

Walk 2

Distance: *Allow three hours for this walk of five miles.*

The tiny car park at the Horseshoe only holds a couple of cars and the pub is extremely busy at weekends, so I advise you arrive early and park along the lane in the village. Taking your leave from the inn turn right along the village lane, shortly to bear off left at the junction by The Old School House and war memorial. Keep left by the telephone box and Old Ford Cottage and bear off right before the entrance to Wake House for the village church. Much of the 15th century church was rebuilt in the 1870s but the grand 400 year old tower, built in the Perpendicular style remains. Unfortunately, our early spring morning start found the church door still locked, but a notice in the lych-gate informed us that the churchyard is a Wildlife Conservation Area. Grasses are left long to help them seed and butterflies to breed and graves and walls are left untouched to preserve mosses.

Leave the churchyard via the lych-gate and turn sharp left to follow a narrow fenced footpath around the perimeter of the churchyard. Good views can be had over the line of pretty thatched cottages into the Ebble Valley and its small lake. When you reach a fork of paths, bear off right downhill to a lane. Turn right, then immediately left along a fenced path which leads you to a footbridge over the Ebble. Winter rain had ensured a constant flow to this intermittent chalk stream and we lingered here to appreciate the early morning peace that shrouded the attractive water meadow scene away to our left.

In a little way cross the stile on your left and follow the worn grassy path that bears diagonally right across the meadow and gently rise uphill away from the river to a stile and a quiet lane. A green footpath fingerpost waymarks your route over the lane and another stile, then turn left along the field edge and begin to climb out of the river valley. Maintain your course left-handed up the field, with fine views back across the serene valley and Ebbesbourne church, until you reach a small wooden gate and blue arrow on your left. Go through the gate and now proceed right-handed along the edge of the field, along a wide grassy path. You are now slowly climbing up onto the high open chalk downland with magnificent vistas opening up across the valley to the line of hills signifying the beginning of Cranborne Chase.

Pass through a metal gate, keep straight ahead up the right-hand edge of hawthorn scrubland to a stile which flanks a horse jump. Your path leads you to a further stile fence and affords glorious views to your right across rolling Prescombe Down and into a fine deep and dry chalk valley. Beyond the stile, bear right onto a wide grassy trackway and gradually ascend to the top of the ridge and a crossroads of tracks. Turn westwards and join the ancient Salisbury Way, once the major routeway between Salisbury and Shaftesbury and the far west. This well established hawthorn-lined drove route leads you across lonely Swallowcliffe Down, an area of open pasture, sheep and skylarks singing high in the skies. One can imagine the travellers in times past — the pilgrims on their way to Shaftesbury and the passengers on the London to Exeter coach — enjoying the summer warmth and scenes from this high vantage point, but in winter this the only route must have been a nightmare journey for there is little or no shelter from the rain and the westerly wind that never ceases to blow.

As you head west a fine panorama presents itself away to the north across the broad, undulating and wooded Nadder Valley. This provides an interesting contrast to the narrow Ebble valley to the south which is dominated by rampart-like chalk downs. A feeling of being away from it all remains with you as you stay on this flinty track, ignoring all waymarked paths on either side. Cross over a metalled lane and pass through a small copse. At the end of the trees, a bridleway is arrowed off to your right, disregard this and look out for the blue arrow on your left, waymarking your path between two posts. It was at this point that we saw two fine Romany caravans camped on the ridgeway. Obviously these peaceful out-of-the-way old tracks have great appeal to these present-day travellers.

You now follow a hedge left-handed along a narrow well-worn path that soon begins to descend the chalk downs, back into the sheltered Ebble Valley. Pass through a copse, then with some splendid rural valley and downland views, head downhill to a small wooden gate. Keep left and descend steeply along a wide chalk trackway towards the magnificent Norrington Manor ahead. When you reach a crossroads of tracks, proceed ahead and pass between a fine collection of barns to where the track veers right to the Manor. Our route passes through the metal gate on your left, but it is worth strolling along the track to view the facade of the partly 14th century stone Manor, once the home of the Gawen family for over 450 years and later the Wyndham clan.

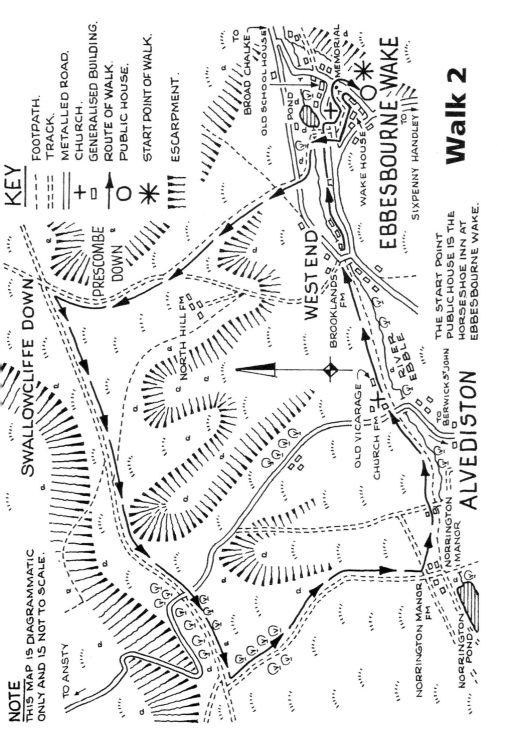

Walk 2

Once you are in the pasture beyond the gate, follow the left-hand wire fence with the narrow grassy impression of the intermittent upper reaches of the River Ebble away to your right. On nearing some cottages, pass to the right of an out-building and cross the driveway to join a narrow defined footpath that runs

Alvediston church — a truly idyllic and tranquil situation

parallel to the infant river and marshy area. Alvediston church soon comes into view ahead as you proceed to a wooden gate and pasture. Keep left-handed along the fence to a stile and metalled lane. Cross over to follow the fingerpost — Ebbesbourne Wake 1m — which points you up the driveway to the Old Vicarage and church. At a metal gate on your right, a painted blue arrow waymarks your path into the riverside meadow.

A short diversion to St. Mary's church is well worth the effort for a number of reasons. Firstly, there are good historical notes explaining the numerous memorials in the church, which relate to the Gawen and Wyndham families. Of particular note is the tomb of a knight in armour, supposedly that of John Gawen. The second reason is to see the tomb of Sir Anthony Eden, who lived in the brick manor to the right of the church. However, in my mind the main incentive to visit the church, is the truly idyllic and tranquil situation that it commands over the now established River Ebble and its lush meadowland. Relax for a few moments, as we did, to appreciate the scene that graces the eye from its tiny porch.

Back on the main route, our path runs through a grassy meadow parallel to the river to a metal gate, beyond which you proceed straight ahead along a defined grass track towards the hamlet of West End. Pass through a black gate and shortly join a track which crosses in front of pretty whitewashed thatched cottage, then goes past a house called 'Badgers Glory' before reaching a lane.

Here you turn right, cross the river, then immediately turn left to follow a lane parallel to the river, passing West End Farm. When you reach the point where the lane bears right uphill, keep ahead at the 'except for access' sign to join a narrow lane. As this lane bears left down towards the river, bear off right at the white railing to follow the narrow path back around Ebbesbourne church to the main village lane, the pub and your transport.

Towpath and footpaths from Little Bedwyn

WALK 3
Allow 3 hours
4 ¹/₂ miles
Walk begins page 20

Background to the Walk

This walk centres on a peaceful stretch of the Kennet and Avon Canal, between Little and Great Bedwyn and its unspoilt surrounding countryside. It was back in 1788 that the idea of linking the River Kennet, which flows into the Thames at Reading, with the River Avon at Bath by means of an artificial waterway was first mooted. The navigation between the rivers had to rise to 450 feet above sea level and needed 104 locks, two aqueducts and, at the summit, a tunnel over 500 yards long. The ambitious project, designed by John Rennie, took 22 years to complete. The canal was used to carry vast quantities of coal, iron, stone and slate, local agricultural products and timber, and to bring luxuries like tobacco and spirits from London.

Transporting goods along the canal proved very successful for 40 years, then with the completion of the railways, offering faster and more efficient transport the canal began to fall into decline. This was despite an effort by the Kennet and Avon Canal Company to build their own railway alongside their canal; they were bought out by the prosperous Great Western Railway Company and this signified the end of the canal. Since 1962 the Kennet and Avon Canal Trust and the Waterways Board have recreated the navigable waterway by clearing the waters and locks for leisure barges and making the banks and towpaths accessible to fishermen, naturalists and walkers.

The starting point of our walk — Little Bedwyn — is split by the canal and railway, with bridges linking each side. On the east side is the old farming community with some pleasant houses that are much older

Maps
Landranger 1:50,000
Sheet 174
Pathfinder 1:25,000
Sheet SU 26/36
Map Reference of Start/
Finish SU292659

How to get there
Little Bedwyn lies a mile off the A4 between Hungerford and Marlborough. From Andover head north from the town centre to join A343 Newbury road. After 5 miles in Hurstbourne Tarrant turn left onto an unclassified lane for Upton and Vernham Dean. Beyond Vernham Dean remain on the lane through Oxenwood, then shortly cross over A338 and in 2 miles enter Great Bedwyn. Turn right in the main street signposted Little Bedwyn. In the village cross the railway and canal and take the next turning right for the Harrow Inn. From Salisbury follow A30 north for Andover and Winchester, then at the second roundabout take the first exit to join A338 for the Winterbournes. Remain on A338, pass beneath A303, go through Shipton Bellinger, Tidworth and Collingbourne Ducis, then after four-and-a-half miles at the junction with B3087 and A346 (Marlborough road), stay on

A338, heading east for Hungerford. After 4 miles take the seventh lane on your left for Great Bedwyn, turning right in the village signed Little Bedwyn.

**Pub facilities
Harrow Inn,
Little Bedwyn**
This excellent Victorian village pub was once tied to the estate and up to 1990 it also served as the Post Office, when the pub closed. Not a drop of ale was served for over a year until a consortium of villagers decided to buy the inn to ensure that their pub remained open. The result is a homely inn with a growing reputation for good home-cooked food and with three en suite bedrooms it is a popular base in which to explore the area. The three inter-connected rooms — all music and game-free — are neat and tidy and simply furnished. The comfortable terracotta painted dining room has varnished pine floorboards, darkwood tables and chairs and tasteful prints and watercolours on the walls. Bar food is served 1200-1400 and 1900-2100 Tuesday to Sunday; restaurant meals from 1930-2100 Wednesday to Saturday and Sunday lunchtimes. Imaginative lunchtime snack choices are chalked up on a blackboard and may include carrot and ginger soup, garlic pate, salmon and herb roulade, satay meatballs with noodles, houmous and hot bread, marinaded veal kebabs and broccoli and parsnip cheese bake. More elaborate and stylish dishes are available in the evenings such as veal, pigeon and pistachio terrine or filo parcels of goat's cheese and herbs for starters, followed by

The Kennet and Avon Canal and Great Bedwyn Church

than the canal. In particular, the 18th century Manor Farmhouse has fine chequered brickwork, a rare octagonal game larder and a collection of interesting barns. The Harrow lies up an adjacent lane. Across the canal and railway, Victorian estate houses line a lane that leads to the partly Norman church of St. Michael. It has a magnificent stone spire rising from a diagonally buttressed flint tower and is a fine landmark in the countryside.

The village nestles in a deep hollow of the hills at an ancient site. A formidable hill-fort — Chisbury Camp — dominates the hills to the west of the village and it is said to derive its name from the early Saxon leader Cissa. Standing within its 50 foot high earth ramparts is the ruined chapel of St. Martin's, now used as a farm building, with windows still bearing 13th century tracery. Leading from here is the Bedwyn Dyke earthworks, which crosses the canal just before Great Bedwyn. It forms one end of the Wansdyke, a linear earthwork that runs from Inkpen through to Bath and on to Bristol. In parts it is a significant feature, but here it is only barely visible.

The larger and more developed village of Great Bedwyn is also situated beside the canal and at one stage was a market town with a borough status, and until the Reform Act of 1832 it had two MPs. The parish in 1866 included a total of 10,420 acres, covering no less

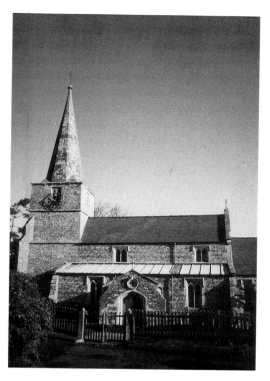

Little Bedwyn Church

chicken breast in black bean sauce, baked skate with a herb crust and calf's liver with smoked bacon and mushrooms. Desserts may include white chocolate meringue with vanilla sauce. A selection of vegetarian dishes are always available. Small brewery real ales are featured here, all served on handpump — Hook Norton Best Bitter, King Alfred's Bitter and Moles Landlord Choice for example. The bar opens from 1100-1430 and 1730-2300 (Saturday from 1800), 1200-1430 and 1900-2230 on Sundays. To the rear of the inn there is a lawned area with picnic benches for al fresco eating. Children, but not dogs, are welcome in the bars.

than seven hamlets and extending to the borders of Savernake Forest. It is still a big parish, but is by no means as important as it was; however it retains the appearance of a small town with a wide main street, continuous rows of cottages and a few elegant town houses set back from the road.

Set in low lying land near the railway and canal is St. Mary's church, one of the largest and finest churches in the area. It dates from the 11th century and was significantly enlarged during the 14th and 15th centuries. In the chancel is the tomb of Sir John Seymour. His daughter Jane was Henry VIII's third wife who died after giving birth to Henry's only son Edward. The tombs and gravestones in the churchyard are dominated by a magnificent cedar tree, its lofty height towering above the splendid church tower and its parapet of open arches.

Gravestones, memorials, fonts, statutory and many other examples of the stonemasons art can be viewed at Lloyds' Stone Museum in Church Street. This fascinating collection traces the history of carved and worked stone of all kinds, including stonemasons' secrets. Many of the tombstones are painted in bright colours, others have curious and amusing rhymes. The museum is run by the seventh generation of a 200-year-old family of stonemasons.

Great Bedwyn was the birthplace of a certain Thomas Willis in 1621. He was Charles II's doctor and with a group of scientists founded the Royal Society. Combining research with a practice and unwearied authorship, he made the first important discovery as to the cause of diabetes and his work on blood flow through the brain was fundamental — a part of the brain is called Willis's Circle.

Walk 3

Distance: *Up to three hours for this four-and-a-half mile walk.*

Parking in the immediate vicinity of the Harrow Inn is limited to a few spaces along the lane. If these are full on your arrival a couple of spaces can be found at the church across the canal and railway. From the Harrow turn left down the lane into the heart of the village and at the crossroads proceed straight across along a dead-end lane towards the canal and railway bridges, passing a house called Old Orchard on your left. In a little way keep to the left of a white gate to join the Kennet and Avon Canal towpath. If you have the time and inclination to explore the west side of the village and the fine Norman church of St. Michael, cross both bridges and bear right. It is worth pausing on the footbridge to appreciate the excellent views along this straight stretch of canal, the colourful narrowboats and well-restored locks.

Our main route heads southwest along the grassy towpath beside Little Bedwyn lock, then passes beneath the road bridge over the canal (under which were moored four brightly painted houseboats) before heading out into peaceful open countryside. The work put in by the Kennet and Avon Canal Trust since 1962 in restoring and maintaining the locks and canal fringes has created a most tranquil habitat for wildlife. Along with the adjacent lush meadowland of the River Dun, birdlife thrives undisturbed and is a haven for breeding Mute Swans, Canada Geese, Mallards, Lapwings, Herons, Kestrels and Wagtails. Your level grassy path, fringed with old pollarded willow trees tracks the reed-edged waters of the canal, passing Potter's Lock with St. Martin's Chapel and the high wooded ramparts of the Iron Age hillfort — Chisbury Camp — dominating the hillside away to your right.

The edge of the much larger settlement of Great Bedwyn is reached as you pass Burnt Mill Lock. The name Bedwyn possibly derives from the Wiltshire dialect word 'bedwine' or 'bedwind', a term used to describe the wild clematis plant which is a native to the county. It has also been linked to a Celtic stream-name of obscure meaning: 'bedewindan' in the Saxon charter dated 778 evidently refers to the small tributary of the Kennet which runs here. The towpath leads you beneath a road bridge, then past the old canal wharf, a scene of great activity when the canal was used to transport coal, for the wharf once housed two coal merchants. Today, the wharf carries out repairs on the leisure narrowboats that cruise the canal.

Beyond the wharf, the large flint church of St. Mary the Virgin and its magnificent Cedar tree begin to dominate the canal-side scene. On reaching Church Lock it is well worth making the short detour over the canal bridge and railway crossing to follow the footpath to the churchyard and possibly to venture further along Church Street to visit the fascinating Stone Museum. Back on the towpath, cross the waymarked stile on your left, opposite the brick canal bridge and bear right, to follow the left-hand line of trees to another stile. A yellow arrow points your way over the stile, then proceed straight ahead, uphill, along the right-hand edge of pasture.

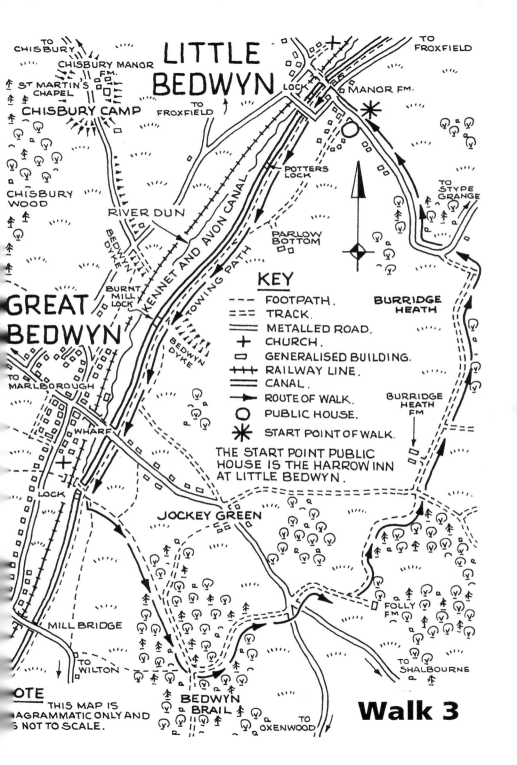

LITTLE BEDWYN

TO CHISBURY
CHISBURY MANOR FM.
St MARTIN'S CHAPEL
CHISBURY CAMP
TO FROXFIELD
TO FROXFIELD
LOCK
MANOR FM.
TO STYPE GRANGE
POTTERS LOCK
CHISBURY WOOD
RIVER DUN
PARLOW BOTTOM
BEDWYN DYKE
KENNET AND AVON CANAL
TOWING PATH
BURNT MILL LOCK
BURRIDGE HEATH

GREAT BEDWYN

BEDWYN DYKE

KEY

- - - FOOTPATH.
=== TRACK.
=== METALLED ROAD.
+ CHURCH.
▢ GENERALISED BUILDING.
+++ RAILWAY LINE.
═ CANAL.
➤ ROUTE OF WALK.
◯ PUBLIC HOUSE.
✳ START POINT OF WALK.

THE START POINT PUBLIC HOUSE IS THE HARROW INN AT LITTLE BEDWYN.

TO MARLBOROUGH
WHARF
LOCK

BURRIDGE HEATH FM.

JOCKEY GREEN

MILL BRIDGE

FOLLY FM.

TO WILTON

TO SHALBOURNE

OTE THIS MAP IS IAGRAMMATIC ONLY AND S NOT TO SCALE.

BEDWYN BRAIL

TO OXENWOOD

Walk 3

Catch your breathe as you near the top of the rise, and absorb the vista that has opened up behind you, along the length of the canal back to Little Bedwyn and its tall church spire and across the village of Great Bedwyn and the fine rural landscape that surrounds it. Your route passes through a gap in the wire fence, beside an old broken stile and maintains its right-hand course along a tree-lined hedgerow towards woodland. On reaching the corner of the field go through a small squeeze stile and enter the woodland. A sign indicates that this is Bedwyn Brail, an extensive area of mixed woodland and asks you to keep to the footpaths and your dog on a lead.

The narrow footpath in front of you leads you through the woodland and shortly emerges out into a clearing. Keep ahead on the defined path and soon bear right where it merges with a wide grassy swath. With a pheasant enclosure to your right and a new plantation of trees on your left, follow this grass thoroughfare, which soon becomes a stony track, to a junction of trackways. Turn left here to join a wide grassy track, which can be rutted and muddy due to the passage of vehicles and disregard all paths that leave this main routeway. You will soon enter into another clearing, keep right-handed along its fringe and shortly meet a trackway that leads you out of Bedwyn Brail.

This established hedged pathway bisects arable fields as it heads eastwards to reach a metalled lane. Turn left, then almost immediately, go straight over at a crossroads into the driveway to Folly Farm. A small footpath marker is visible on the farm sign. Follow the driveway round to the right towards the main house, then bear off left uphill with the blue arrow, along a grassy track. Your route passes in front of Folly Farm, gently rising uphill before bearing left away from the farm. Keep ahead across grassland towards a post situated at the base of a copse. The arrow on the post directs you around the left-hand side of the copse, where you keep to the edge of the copse and coniferous plantation beyond. A white arrow will soon reassure you that you are heading in the right direction.

On reaching the corner of the field go through the narrow section of scrub and trees into the crop field beyond. You now turn right to follow the perimeter of the field round to a muddy track. Turn right again, then at the junction in front of you bear left along a pitted metalled track towards Burridgeheath Farm, which lies to your left. Remain on this quiet traffic-free tarmacadamised byway to where it merges with a country lane. Turn left here to follow the lane gently downhill for half-a-mile, with good valley views ahead, back into Little Bedwyn and The Harrow Inn.

Border paths and tracks from Lower Chute

WALK 4
At least 3 hours
6 miles
Walk begins page 25

Background to the Walk

This walk explores the hilly and relatively deserted border country between Wiltshire and Hampshire, in what remains of Chute Forest. In medieval times vast tracts of forest canopied an area stretching from Savernake Forest to Salisbury and swelling out again into the New Forest and provided a prime hunting ground for Norman and medieval kings. The Domesday Book records that nearby Collingbourne Ducis had a wood 'one league long and as much broad in a third part of the wood called Cetum' (Chute).

The parishes of Chute and Chute Forest can be traced back to Norman times and it is assumed that the ancient meaning of Chute is wood, or forest. Habitation within the parishes at that time may well have been no more than a few cottages in a large clearing occupied by charcoal burners or peasants. Deforestation began in 1632 during the reign of Charles I, who divided the area up among favoured nobles. The result of this is still evident today, for there is no village in the generally accepted sense of the word, but a collection of five small hamlets — Upper, Lower, Chute Standen, Chute Forest and Chute Cadley — which developed around what were once farms or country houses, such as Standen House and Chute Lodge.

The last Warden, or Ranger of Chute Forest, was Sir John Philpot, who died in 1662. He was given authority to preserve the game 'in the forest and within seven miles compass of the same'. After the deforestation, Sir John received from the King a grant of lands worth £600 in compensation, which gives a good indication of the value of the position he had.

Maps
Landranger 1:50,000
Sheet 185
Pathfinder 1:25,000
Sheet SU 25/35
Map Reference of Start/
Finish SU311532

How to get there
The hamlet of Lower Chute is located in a very rural area north of Andover. From Andover town centre follow the Ring Road west for A303 Exeter, eventually reaching the roundabout that precedes A303 and take the fifth exit to join A342 Devizes road. After 1·5 miles, just beyond the church in Weyhill, turn right for Clanville and Tangley and remain on this lane for 3·5 miles to take the third lane on your left signed Lower Chute. The Hatchet lies on the right in the hamlet. From Salisbury follow signs M3, A30 London and Andover out of the centre and head north eastwards soon to merge with A343 towards Andover. Approaching Andover A343 merges with A303, head westwards exiting at the next junction to cross A303 towards the town centre. At the roundabout beyond A303 take the first exit to join A342 Devizes road, then follow directions explained above.

Pub facilities
Hatchet, Lower Chute
(Pictured far right)
*Situated among a web of
narrow lanes, this idyllic
thatched country pub is an
ideal spot from which to start
walking. Built in the 16th
century as three cottages, it is
full of charm and atmosphere
with a heavily-beamed low
ceiling and an enormous
inglenook, with log fire, that
takes up a whole wall — an
ideal place to while away a
winter lunchtime or evening.
This main bar also has bench
and pew seating, a mix of
captains and wheel-back chairs
and an array of old prints and
horsebrasses on the walls. A
small snug area is simply
furnished and with various
farming memorabilia adorning
the walls. The relaxing rural
feel to the pub is maintained
in the intimate, low-ceilinged
restaurant. A well stocked bar
features four real ales such as
Gales HSB, Wadworth 6X,
Bass and Charrington IPA
and are available from 1100-
1500 and 1800-2300 and
during the usual Sunday
opening times. The bar food
menu is chalked up on a
blackboard and changes daily,
offering such hearty fare as
split pea soup, spaghetti
Bolognaise, steak and kidney
pie, smoked trout or French-
style pate, lamb Madras,
chicken tandoori, fried
calamares, venison sausage
casserole and local game from
nearby estates — venison pie
and jugged hare in season.
Good ploughmans and a range
of sandwiches are also
available at lunchtimes.
Vegetarian choices may
include spinach and tomato
lasagne and cauliflower and
courgette bake. More formal*

There are two churches within the parishes, one of which — St. Mary's — built at the end of the last century for the nearby mansion of Chute Lodge, now belongs to the Redundant Churches Fund. A service is held once a year in the summer, yet its bells will not peal to herald the congregation, for they were removed in 1976 and installed in St. Nicholas' church in Upper Chute. The hamlet of Upper Chute is by far the largest of the settlements, located around a tidy green and the junction of five lanes. Amenities are limited within the area to a village hall, which was once the school and two pubs — The Hatchet in Lower Chute and The Cross Keys in Upper Chute.

The landscape is still well wooded with a mixture of copse, plantations, windbreaks or 'rows' and roadside plantings of beech linked by a sprinkling of hedgerow trees. The paths and byways chosen for this walk explore in depth this quite remote area of Wiltshire, which rises to over 800 feet, affording splendid views south across Hampshire to the Isle of Wight.

The highest point of our walk is along the impressive Chute Causeway, which was originally part of the Roman highway from Winchester to Mildenhall. It forms a great arc around some of the most attractive scenery in Wiltshire, for just north of the now paved road are deep combes and steep hills. These hills are so steep that the Roman road, which usually ignores natural obstacles, swerves to avoid the deep combe, known as Hippenscombe Bottom. At the far end of the Causeway is Conholt House, a large, early 19th century building of grey brick. It was here in 1898, during excavations, that a six foot wide terrace set with 12-16 inches of flints, covered with layers of soil, clay and compacted chalk and finished with finer flints set by hand were uncovered. A few of these had the appearance of having been burnt, which offered an explanation to the way the Romans straightened their roads. By lighting fires at both ends of the semi-circular section of the causeway they could line up the columns of smoke to re-align their road.

While walking this lonely stretch of road look out for a ghost — the Causeway is haunted by a priest with figurative blood on his hands.

meals are served in the cosy restaurant. Both bar and restaurant food are available daily from 1200-1400 and 1900-2200 (2130 on Sundays), although the restaurant is closed on Sunday and Monday evenings. Children are not allowed into the pub but there is a side lawn with play area and a front terrace lined with picnic benches. Dogs are welcome in the main bar. Walkers may leave their cars in the pub's car park if permission is asked first.

Walk 4

Distance: *Up to three hours for this six mile walk*

Having prized yourself away from the Hatchet, cross the gravel car park and turn left along the peaceful lane that passes through this idyllic hamlet. Follow the lane around to the right passing the war memorial, the small green and an attractive thatched cottage — Elm Cottage, then bear off right onto a waymarked bridleway which skirts the garden of a bungalow. The blue arrow directs you to the side of a gate, then along a narrow path between paddock and wire fencing, which dog-legs right then left to a metal gate. The steeple of St. Mary's church can be seen looming above the copse ahead.

Beyond the gate, your route keeps right-handed along the edge of a tranquil and lush grassy valley, known as Cadley Bottom. Follow the fence towards Great Lodge Copse, pass through a field entrance, then on reaching a small wooden gate on your right, enter the copse. Keep left at the immediate fork of paths and follow the gently rising narrow earth path through the predominantly hazel woodland, towards St. Mary's church which soon comes into view. Our rather cold February day ramble through this copse was brightened up the beautiful large clumps of snowdrops that seemed to thrive in this peaceful spot.

Your woodland path soon emerges out onto a wide grassy track. From here, go straight across to an old wooden gate and enter the churchyard to St. Mary's church — a good reason for initially venturing south from Lower Chute. The church was built at the end of the last century, but has been redundant since the early 1970s, its six bells having been transferred to St. Nicholas's church in Upper Chute in 1976. The brick and flint church enjoys an isolated spot at the end of a little lane and once served the nearby mansion in Chute Forest. The churchyard is delightfully wild, full of yew and clumps of snowdrops and other early spring flowers on our visit, but I can imagine it to be abundant with flora and fauna in the summer months due to its undisturbed nature. Unfortunately the church doors were locked, but those of you who are keen to explore its redundant treasures can obtain the key at nearby Kiln House.

Leave the churchyard by the way you came in, turn left and immediately pass through a large five-barred wooden gate, then keep right with the waymarked footpath sign to follow a wide trackway northwards alongside scrub and woodland. The track soon bears left with the fence, away from the trees and leads you to a small wooden gate. Follow the line of trees and field edge left-handed towards the playing field visible ahead. Climb a stile, join a grass centred track and pass to the left of the playing field to reach a lane, opposite a picturesque whitewashed thatched cottage called Fox Cottage. Turn right, then just before the playground sign bear off left onto an established footpath to the left of a house which becomes lined with a holly hedgerow and wooden fencing as you proceed towards two white cottages. Your path takes you close to the cottages, then passes between tree-lined hedgerows with good views away to your right down into the valley towards Chute Standen.

Shortly, emerge from the trees and bear slightly left with the yellow footpath sign to follow a defined grassy path left-handed along the perimeter of a field, with the Hampshire-style spire of St. Nicholas's church in view straight ahead. To your right across the field and in a splendid rural setting is the old village school. Easily recognisable as a school, this fine brick and flint building closed in 1978 after a century of educating the local children, but it still serves the community, now as a village hall. At the end of this grassy thoroughfare, turn left along a quiet lane — Malthouse Lane — following it into the hamlet of Upper Chute, where you keep right at the central green and telephone box towards the church.

St. Nicholas church was built between 1869-1872 by the eminent Victorian architect J. L. Pearson and stands on the site of an ancient church, consecrated in 1325. The only surviving relic of the original church is a badly damaged memorial stone by the chancel gates, which records the death in 1792 of Sir Sidney Meadows, Knight Marshal of England, who lived at Conholt Park in the 18th century. Other treasures are linked to the Wellesley family who also resided at Conholt House in later years.

Back on the lane, turn right to follow it around the churchyard, then go round a sharp left-hand bend, shortly to pass a junction and farmhouse on your left. Gently climb uphill for a little way before turning right at the bridleway fingerpost, which points your way along a wide grass centred stony track. Your route undulates eastwards, soon becoming tree-lined and skirting a small copse, which on a fine late spring day will be carpeted with bluebells. Cross straight over a narrow lane, the blue bridleway sign arrowing your course along a further wide byway, lined to your right with holly and beech. As you head gradually downhill, Standen House comes into view through the trees on your right, then at the base of the hill disregard the track branching off to the right and maintain your easterly direction, uphill along this established beech-lined track known as Breach Lane.

When you reach a fork in the track with a private thoroughfare and woods

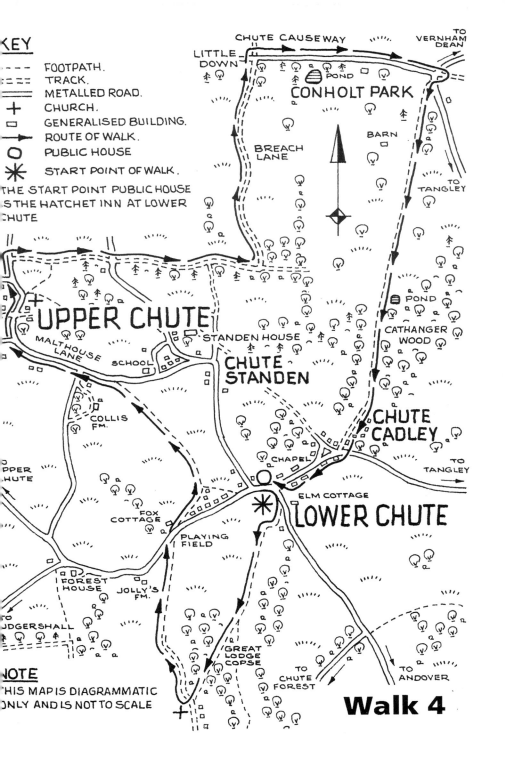

KEY

- - - FOOTPATH.
≡≡≡ TRACK.
═══ METALLED ROAD.
✝ CHURCH.
▢ GENERALISED BUILDING.
➡ ROUTE OF WALK.
Ọ PUBLIC HOUSE
✳ START POINT OF WALK.

THE START POINT PUBLIC HOUSE
IS THE HATCHET INN AT LOWER
CHUTE

CHUTE CAUSEWAY
TO VERNHAM DEAN
LITTLE DOWN
POND
CONHOLT PARK
BREACH LANE
BARN
TO TANGLEY

UPPER CHUTE
MALTHOUSE LANE
SCHOOL
STANDEN HOUSE
CHUTE STANDEN
CATHANGER WOOD
POND

COLLIS FM.

CHUTE CADLEY
TO TANGLEY

UPPER CHUTE

CHAPEL

ELM COTTAGE
LOWER CHUTE

FOX COTTAGE
PLAYING FIELD

FOREST HOUSE
JOLLY'S FM.

TO LUDGERSHALL

GREAT LODGE COPSE

TO CHUTE FOREST
TO ANDOVER

NOTE

THIS MAP IS DIAGRAMMATIC
ONLY AND IS NOT TO SCALE

Walk 4

ahead, bear sharp left with the main track to begin a long gradual climb northwards up to Little Down and Chute Causeway. With hedges on both sides, Breach Lane is a fine old green way that divides open stretches of farmland and affords delightful rural views south across rolling Hampshire downland, as you ascend to over 800 feet above sea level at the Causeway. At the end of this track pass through a small metal gate, then turn right onto a quiet metalled lane — Chute Causeway. This impressive Roman road, which once linked Winchester to Mildenhall, curves round the deep hollow of Hippenscombe and the hillfort of Fosbury, which dominates Knolls Down beyond. Both these and the splendid panoramas south can be appreciated as you make your way along this straight ridge road. The open downland area along the length of this ancient road here is littered with old tracks, field ditches, tumulli, long barrows and pit dwellings.

Old village pump at Upper Chute Church

The Causeway soon leads you to T-junction, opposite the driveway to Conholt House and the point where the Roman road returns to its southerly course towards Winchester. Your route crosses a rickety stile, located next to a gate to your right, a yellow arrow waymarking the path across Conholt Park. The footpath is by no means defined through the open parkland, so keep left of the large fir tree and the holly tree beyond, then maintain a course that heads well left of the metal barn visible ahead and eventually reach a stile in the fence on a line parallel to the barn. Cross the stile and proceed ahead — not half-right as the wayward yellow arrow indicates — to a further stile in wire fencing. From here we had to bear half-right for a short distance to skirt a patch of old kale, before resuming our southerly direction to a field entrance strung with a temporary wire and pole fence. The stile flanking it was in a sorry state of repair and unusable.

Once in the pasture beyond your path follows the right-hand fence and this peaceful stretch of the walk yielded an interesting abundance of wildlife, which included a couple of hares, rabbits, pheasants and a buzzard soaring high above Cathanger Wood to the left. Pass a water trough and a small tree-ringed pond, then continue right-handed with the yellow footpath markers on posts alongside the woodland. On reaching a metal gate, climb the stile to its left, then follow the arrowed woodland edged track ahead and shortly merge with a grass-cum-gravel driveway. Proceed straight on past a wooden building and stabling towards some cottages and the edge of Chute Cadley. Your route becomes metalled, then at a T-junction turn right and walk downhill into Lower Chute, keeping left at the next junction to pass Well Cottage and later the wooden Methodist Chapel on your right as you make your way back to the small village green. Pass the war memorial and bear right back to The Hatchet.

Forest tracks and Anton Valley paths from Upper Clatford

Background to the Walk

The River Anton rises just north of the market town of Andover and meanders through the town centre before merging with its tributary, Pillhill Brook at Upper Clatford. From here this delightful chalk stream flows south eastwards through unspoilt meadowland, eventually swelling the waters of the Test at Fullerton. The attractive collection of predominantly thatched houses that form the village of Upper Clatford, nestle beside the clear waters of the Anton, yet the village is perilously close to the centre of Andover — one-and-a-quarter miles to be precise.

The name Clatford has an unusual meaning — 'ford where burdock grew'. The history of the village can be traced back to the Iron Age, for on Bury hill overlooking the valley is a hill-fort which was abandoned in about AD100. Unlike neighbouring Danebury Ring little is known about it, as the most recent excavations, in the 1930s, were inconclusive.

A famous feature of the valley and village was an ironworks, founded in 1813 by Robert Tasker and first located in Abbots Ann. It later moved to Upper Clatford and was renamed the Waterloo Ironworks, manufacturing pumps, agricultural machinery and other wrought-iron tools. It became famous for its traction engines, the first being completed in 1869 and later, during the Second World War, made thousands of aircraft trailers. When the works closed many of its tools were acquired by Andover Museum who set up a permanent display on the firm. Three reminders of the works survive; Waterloo Workmens' Hall (1867), now the Waterloo Free Church, a terrace of foundry

Maps
Landranger 1:50,000
Sheet 185
Pathfinder 1:25,000
Sheets SU 24/34 & SU 44/45
Map Reference of Start/
Finish SU355437

How to get there
Upper Clatford is located only one-and-a-quarter miles south of Andover. From the town centre follow A3057 south for Romsey, taking the first right, signed Upper Clatford, after crossing over A303. Soon turn left across the River Anton, pass the church and go over a brick bridge before turning right into the village. Village hall and pub lie on your left. From Salisbury follow signs 'M3, A30, A343 London and Andover' and head north eastwards to join A30. In 7 miles keep ahead on A343 for Andover, then on nearing the town pass a turning on your left for Abbotts Ann before taking next right for Anna Valley and The Clatfords and follow this into Upper Clatford. Hampshire Bus 99 between Andover and Stockbridge stops in Upper Clatford and Wherwell. Wilts & Dorset/Hants. Buses 7, 8 and 9, Hants. Bus service 76/76A and frequent trains link Salisbury with Andover.

Pub facilities
Crook and Shears,
Upper Clatford

This attractive pub, built at the end of the 16th century, occupies a central position in the village. Reputedly haunted by a teenage girl, daughter of a landlord back in the mid 1600s. She fell pregnant by the local vicar and died while giving birth at the pub. I was told that cats and dogs will not enter this room because of her ghostly presence. The interior is simple and cosy, the lounge bar being warmed by a log fire situated in a huge brick inglenook fireplace. The Saddle Room public bar is available for private functions and has a skittle alley. A sheltered courtyard and pleasant beer garden make ideal spots during fine weather. Good range of real ales await thirsty walkers, such as Flowers, Boddingtons, Castle Eden Ale, Brakspears and a guest ale — Hogs Back on my visit. Snacks and more substantial meals are served in the bar. Choose from a range of sandwiches, ploughmans, filled jacket potatoes, salads, a bowl of soup served with crusty bread, pate and toast, garlic toast, hot mackerel and egg mayonnaise. Larger appetites are offered home-baked steak and kidney pie, ham, egg and chips, roast chicken and chips, macaroni cheese, ravioli or one of the authentic daily curries. Food served from 1200-1500 (1430 on Sunday) and 1800-2100 (from 1900 on Sunday). Bar opens Monday-Friday from 1100-1500 and 1730-2300, Saturdays from 1100-2300, usual hours on Sundays. Children and dogs are very welcome.

The Crook and Shears at Upper Clatford

workers' houses known as Waterloo Terrace and a pretty little cast-iron bridge spanning the Anton with '1843' and 'Taskers' cast into its metalwork.

Part of our walk explores Harewood Forest, a remnant of a much larger tract of woodland that once cloaked the high downs of north Hampshire and extended into Wiltshire. In days past it has been a royal hunting ground and more recently an ammunition storage area during the Second World War. Nowadays the forest is a peaceful place to explore, across a network of footpaths through mixed woodland. Of all the footpaths that criss-cross Harewood Forest, the Test Way is the best-known and most walked.

From Harewood Forest our walk follows the well defined and clearly marked route of the Test Way and leads you into the picture postcard village of Wherwell It is an odd name, first recorded in AD955 as 'Hwerwyl' meaning 'cauldron springs', but it is the pronunciation of the word that creates the problems. Strangers to the area speak the word as it is spelt, but to the locals the village is 'Whirrell', 'Wurrell', 'Hurrell' or 'Werral'.

Wherwell was the scene of great Saxon intrigue and treachery which ended in murder. In the 960s, King Edgar owned the manor and heard about the charms of a lady called Elfrida. He sent a trusted courtier to report on her beauty, with a view to marrying her. The courtier sent false reports back to the King and married her himself. When the deceit was discovered Edgar murdered him while out hunting in Harewood Forest. Edgar later married Elfrida who bore him a son, Ethelred. The King already had a son, Edward, from a previous marriage who was heir to the throne. Elfrida arranged for the murder of Edward at Corfe Castle four years later, so that Ethelred could take the crown. Ethelred's reign was a disaster and Elfrida, as an act of penitence, founded a nunnery in Wherwell and died there in 1002.

The nunnery was replaced following the Dissolution with a priory and became the family seat of the De La Warrs. Both buildings were located near the church as is the present priory, a handsome early 19th century house. Fragments of the original buildings can be traced, but much of the stone was used in the Church of St. Peter and some carved pieces can be found in a farm wall.

Walk 5

Distance: *Allow a good four-and-a-half hours for this eight mile ramble.*

The Crook and Shears, tucked as it is in a row of cottages has limited parking space, so it is best to park your car in the village hall car park if the roadside spaces outside the inn are full. On leaving the pub turn right along the village street and head gently downhill to where a signpost directs you left along a lane towards All Saints church. Almost immediately cross the large brick bridge over the peacefully meandering River Anton and its lush watermeadow scenes. To your right is a small lake which provides a haven for geese and ducks, while on your left is the 12th century church with a delightful line of lime trees leading to its 18th century brick porch.

Remain on the lane and cross over a further river channel near a cottage, then bear right at a T-junction of lanes, shortly to pass a house and a complex of outbuildings. Just beyond these a footpath fingerpost points your way right across a stile flanking a metal gate. A stony drive leads you past the collection of old barns, your path soon becoming narrow and fenced running parallel to the driveway to River Place. Soon climb a stile on your left, cross the driveway, your route being waymarked between a hedge and a wire fence to a further stile, then proceed ahead along a track beside a garage. Your path becomes grassy as you make your way to a stile in a wooden fence and a HCC official diversion sign, which arrows you over the stile onto a narrow defined path along a line of trees and around River Place estate.

Pass to the left of a couple of paddocks, then on reaching a metalled lane turn right to pass a bungalow and cottages. On reaching the main drive to Meadow Lodge, take the waymarked path through a kissing gate on your left and follow the pathway along the right-hand edge of a crop field, parallel to a stream. Beyond a further kissing gate in the corner of the field, keep straight on across pasture with Goodworth Clatford church away to your left. This grass path leads through two more kissing gates to a lane, where you turn left to pass St. Peters church.

St. Peter's has been altered and extended since it was first built in the 12th century and has a plain 14th century tower and Victorian spire. Inside, there are thick Norman pillars, a Norman table-type font of Purbeck marble. When the chancel was stripped in 1979, a 'workman's doodle' in the form of a miniature carving was found. It is now in the window reveal behind the vicar's desk.

Taking your leave from the church follow the lane to where it joins the busy A3057, then taking great care go straight across onto a waymarked footpath. Pass through a metal kissing gate and begin your gradual climb uphill along a delightful hedged chalk trackway to a T-junction of established routes. Turn right onto a wide bridleway, its hedgerows thick with brambles and proceed in a southerly direction, shortly to pass beneath overhead electricity cables, then in a little way at a woodland fringe, turn left and keep left to follow a well worn path along the edge of Upping Copse. Open undulating farmland sweeps away from the perimeter of this predominantly oak, beech and hazel wood, which is carpeted with a mass of bluebells in the height of spring. Your path will soon cross the entrance to a track leading to an isolated gamekeepers cottage (fronted by numerous pens containing hens and guinea fowl) and becomes a wide, grassy track parallel to the woodland fringe.

This peaceful thoroughfare eventually merges with a concrete farm road, keep left and head towards the large tract of woodland that confronts you. Where the farm road bears left, just as you enter the trees, lookout for a footpath sign partly obscured within a bush and veer off right to join a well used track that passes initially between a small copse of silver birch and oak woodland. You are now entering Harewood Forest, an area of unspoilt woodland that is haven to a diverse collection of wildlife, particularly noted for the carpets of bluebells in spring. Your track soon emerges out into a broad avenue that probes deeper into this predominantly deciduous woodland. Keep your eyes peeled and your voices low, for you may see deer here at any time of the day.

On reaching a crossroads of tracks go straight on through an old gateway to pass through what was an enclosure on a narrower path. We walked this way in early February and the generally drab winter woodland scene was brightened up by the presence of vast clumps of snowdrops. A further disused gateway leads you out to an area of dumped rubble, beyond which you join a muddy trackway and the route of the long distance footpath known as the Test Way. Turn right uphill to a group of outbuildings belonging to Park Farm, then at a post with the Test Way arrow and logo bear right onto a wide trail around the back of disused pig pens. Your route now follows the Test Way over a crossroads of paths, then along the left-hand fringe of woodland on a defined trackway which shortly bears left around open farmland to a junction of tracks at the end of the woodland.

The green arrow points your way ahead, the Test Way becoming a tree-lined track bisecting arable fields as it drops downhill towards a bungalow and fine old barn. On reaching New Barn keep left with the TW sign and gently climb uphill along the grass-centred track between lines of trees before descending what

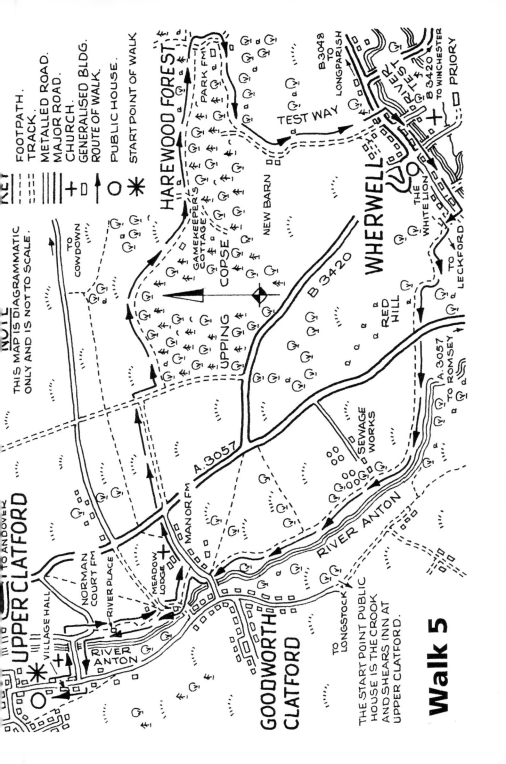

KEY
FOOTPATH.
TRACK.
METALLED ROAD.
MAJOR ROAD.
CHURCH.
GENERALISED BLDG.
ROUTE OF WALK.
PUBLIC HOUSE.
START POINT OF WALK.

NOTE
THIS MAP IS DIAGRAMMATIC
ONLY AND IS NOT TO SCALE.

HAREWOOD FOREST

PARK FM.

B.3048
TO
LONGPARISH

TEST WAY

B.3420
TO WINCHESTER

PRIORY

NEW BARN

WHERWELL

GAMEKEEPER'S COTTAGE

THE WHITE LION

TO COWDOWN

UPPING COPSE

B.3420

RED HILL

TO LECKFORD

A.3057

A.3057
TO ROMSEY

MANOR FM.

A.3057

SEWAGE WORKS

RIVER ANTON

UPPER CLATFORD

TO ANDOVER

VILLAGE HALL

NORMAN COURT FM.

RIVER PLACE

MEADOW LODGE

RIVER ANTON

GOODWORTH CLATFORD

TO LONGSTOCK

THE START POINT PUBLIC
HOUSE IS THE CROOK
AND SHEARS INN AT
UPPER CLATFORD.

Walk 5

becomes an old sunken lane to a gate. Pass to the side of the gate, keep ahead where the track splits and soon reach the B3048 and the edge of Wherwell. Here you turn right to follow the road into the centre of this most picturesque of Hampshire villages. Characterised by a wealth of black and white and heavily thatched cottages, especially along the tiny lane leading to the church on your left, this 'chocolate box' village enjoys a beautiful setting close to the River Test.

It is worth lingering awhile to visit the parish church of St. Peter and Holy Cross in the meadows, for it displays a few fragments of stone from the ancient Priory that once existed here. A newer priory, a 19th century house close to the church, is now home to the Countess of Brecknock and is not open to the public. Proceed through the village and keep straight on where the B-road bears right uphill by the White Lion, to follow the lane towards Fullerton. A fine collection of individually styled houses line your route as you head south-westwards parallel to the river. An interesting diversion can be made when you reach the Test Way sign and path leading to a footbridge over the Test on your left. It is the best opportunity on this walk to view the clear waters of this famous trout stream and to explore the delightful unspoilt watermeadows beyond — if you so desire.

Our main route remains on the lane, disregarding the Test Way which is the first path arrowed to your right and proceeds a little further to a blue arrowed bridleway located opposite an unusual Gothic-style house. Turn right, go through a small gate, then pass under the brick bridge to the now disused Hurstbourne to Fullerton railway line before bearing left along a defined track around the perimeter of a field. Gradually climb uphill, bear left with the fence and savour the good views across the serene Test Valley that have opened up behind you. At the top of the rise the track bears right, becoming hedged as it heads gently downhill to enter a field. Keep right-handed around the field edge, this time with views into the Anton valley, to a small wooden gate, then follow the narrow earth path across the scrub covered hillside to a fork in the path and turn right to follow the wire fence to a footpath fingerpost. This directs you steeply downhill into the valley to a field gate that precedes the busy A3057.

Carefully cross the road and pass through a metal gate into a field and follow the wide arrowed bridleway along the left-hand edge of a large field, with the River Anton visible away to your left. In the far corner of the field go through a further metal gate, then ignore the waymarked path to your left and proceed through a copse and along the left-hand perimeter of the field beyond. Eventually your path enters woodland and tracks the banks of the River Anton. Emerge from the trees and maintain your course parallel to the peaceful river and its associated meadow scenes to a metal kissing gate and a further wooded riverside area. The established path heads towards Goodworth Clatford, now visible ahead and brings you to a gate and a lane. Turn right along the lane and follow it towards St. Peter's church to pick up your outward route that links the two Clatford villages. Retrace your steps back to your car.

Ebble Valley footpaths from Nunton

WALK 6
Allow 2 hours
4 miles
Walk begins page 38

Background to the Walk

The River Ebble or Chalkebourne as it is also known is a tiny clear chalk stream that rises near Alvediston, close to Cranborne Chase and gently flows eastwards through a string of picturesque villages for thirteen miles before merging with the River Avon at Bodenham, south of Salisbury. The valley it has created is the most peaceful and unspoilt of all the fine chalk valleys that radiate from the majestic city of Salisbury. It remains secluded, bordered both to the north and south by high chalk downs and their ancient ridgeway paths and thankfully the tranquil rural scenes are free from the intrusion of busy roads.

The village of Nunton lies close to where the crystal clear waters of the Ebble drain into the much larger Avon. At one time Nunton and nearby Bodenham formed a parish in their own right and was closely linked with Longford Castle Estate and the Radnor family, who in years past owned all the valley land up to Combe Bissett. In 1934 both these communities were incorporated in the parish of Odstock. Longford Castle is a triangular house of 16th century origin and is one of the county's finest country houses, set in 250 acres of landscaped park and gardens, laid out by Capability Brown. The Radnor family still reside in the house and the last remaining link with the family in Nunton is preserved in the name of the village pub — The Radnor Arms. The house and gardens are open by appointment only.

Nunton has a predominantly Victorian church and an 18th century manor house with some fine gardens. It was built by a wealthy merchant from Salisbury who

Maps
Landranger 1:50,000
Sheet 184
Pathfinder 1:25,000
Sheet SU 02/12
Map Reference of Start/
Finish SU158261

How to get there
From Salisbury town centre head south to join A338 towards Fordingbridge and Ringwood. After 2 miles turn right signposted Nunton, the village lies just off the main road. From Andover follow A3057 for Stockbridge/ Romsey, then shortly head west along A303 for 1 mile to join the A343 for Salisbury. Merge with A30, enter Salisbury and follow 'through traffic' signs south to join A338 Ringwood road. Wilts and Dorset bus service 29 from Salisbury to Shaftesbury via the Chalke valley passes through Odstock village and services X3 (to Bournemouth), 43 and 44 (to Downton) stop at both Odstock and Nunton. Hampshire Bus and Wilts and Dorset services 7, 8, 9 and Hampshire Bus service 76 link Andover to Salisbury as does a fast rail service.

Pub facilities
Radnor Arms
(Pictured right)
*The main bar of this
unpretentious ivy-clad pub
dates from the 1670s while the
side part of the pub was once a
post office and general store.
The original low-ceilinged bar
is neatly furnished and is
warmed by a large brick
fireplace and wood burning
stove. Beyond is a larger more
recent open-plan area
overlooking a peaceful garden
and meadows. A tiny public
bar has a quarry-tiled floor
and bar billiards. Hall and
Woodhouse stock their Best
Bitter, Tanglefoot and Hard
Tackle as well as Charles
Wells Bombardier are served
on handpump and available
from 1100-1500 and 1800-
2300 (usual hours on
Sunday). The selection of
lunchtime food includes a
range of ploughmans, filled
jacket potatoes, steak & kidney
pie, a curry plus a daily
specials board which may
feature pan fried sardines,
fresh mussels, lasagne, lamb
tikka, grilled lamb chop, a
choice of salads, quiches and
steaks. Puddings include
treacle and walnut tart, apple
pie, mincemeat pie and bread
& butter. A more elaborate
menu is available in the
evening ranging from avocado
soup and smoked trout to
chicken and mushroom
tagliatelle, rack of lamb, duck
breast and fresh fish dishes.
Sunday lunch booking is
advisable. Meals are served
from 1200-1400 (1330 on
Sunday) and 1900-2130.
Children are welcome in the
side room and have their own
menu to choose from. Dogs
only allowed in the public bar.*

fell in love with a local farming girl. She would only marry him if he built a house that was within sight of her mother's. This he duly did in order to please his bride, but built the house facing away from her mother's farm.

The attractive collection of houses that form the village of Odstock lie at a crossroads where an ancient drove road meets the valley route and crosses the Ebble. This old highway linked Southampton Water with Old Sarum and is known as The Cloven Way. It can be traced up a fine ride of mature beech trees — The Avenue — which heads south up onto Odstock Down from the Manor House in the village. At the end of the Avenue the drove enters Odstock Copse. Here there is a double line of semi-circular banks or earthworks where the Saxons would have kept their flocks sheltered before they continued their journey.

Dominating the landscape around Odstock and crowning Clearbury Down at a height of 468 feet is Clearbury Ring, an ancient Iron Age earth rampart topped with beech trees and undisturbed scrubland. Not far away, close to an area of Stone Age long barrows and Iron Age boundaries such as Grims Ditch which extends some 14 miles through the heart of Cranborne Chase, is the old forests of Great Yews and Little Yews. It is thought the name of the fine timber framed and thatched Yew Tree Inn in Odstock is associated with these two magnificent plantations.

The church of St. Mary's in Odstock lies detached a

Yew Tree Inn *(left)*
This black and white timbered and thatched inn enjoys a good reputation in the area for its location and food. Relax in the neat front garden, complete with picnic benches and huge yew tree or on winter days settle in front of the open log fire with a pint of Gibbs Mew Wiltshire Bitter, Premium, the stronger Bishops Tipple or draught Bass. The huge brick fireplace is fronted with a mix of captains and wheel-backed chairs and padded bench seating. The low-ceilinged bar and small restaurant area have a cosy atmosphere, ideal in which to savour the choice of meals that are chalked up on the blackboard above the fireplace. Snacks include salads, sandwiches and ploughmans with more hearty fare ranging from Yew Tree mixed grill, fresh grilled plaice, sausage casserole, rabbit and pheasant casserole to a 14oz T-bone steak and a choice of vegetarian dishes — tagliatelle and cream cheese bake and macaroni cheese. The restaurant selection may feature game casserole, whole roast squab pigeon, veal masala or pike steak.

one edge of the village street, yet is in close proximity to the manor house. Its was largely rebuilt in the 1870s in flint and stone, but its interior still has traces of Norman work in one of its chancel windows. The treasure of the church however, is the pulpit, which has panels carved with Tudor roses and marigolds and one panel with a painted crown and Queen Elizabeth I initials and the date 1580.

The church and the village is also well known for the Odstock Curse. In the southeast corner of the church-yard is the grave of a legendary local figure, Joshua Scamp, a gypsy who was wrongfully hanged for horse-stealing in 1801. Scamp became a martyr among his people, and each year they assembled around his grave on the anniversary of his death, after first drinking lengthily to his memory in the Yew Tree Inn. One year, the rector and his churchwardens decided to stop the riotous behaviour by locking the church door and uprooting a briar rose which the gypsies had planted by Scamp's grave. The thwarted gypsies put a curse on anyone who should in future lock the door and, after sudden death befell two who defied the curse, the rector threw the key into the Ebble, where it is said still to be.

Beyond the village of Odstock our walk explores the peaceful meadows and paths on the northern side of the River Ebble. The walker is totally unaware of the proximity of the built-up residential area of Salisbury which lies over the hill. The sight of Odstock Hospital on top of the down is the only indication. The hospital is well known for its pioneering work in plastic surgery. On the hill near the hospital is the site of a once prosperous farmstead, the Iron Age 'village' of Little Woodbury. The settlement would have contained a large wooden roundhouse with a high, east-facing gateway, allowing good visibility across the valley.

Walk 6

Distance: *Allow up to two hours for this four mile walk*

Turn left along the lane away from the Radnor Arms for a short distance until you reach a small parking area on your left. Cross the lane and walk up the grassy area (not waymarked) beside the walled garden to a house called The Cottage and cross the lawn via two wooden kissing-gates, then proceed towards the tiny village church on a well-worn path across pasture. Pass through the metal swing gate into the churchyard and bear right round to the main door, which was unfortunately locked when we tried the handle, then leave the churchyard by the main gate and follow the gravel drive up to a lane. Here turn left passing Church Cottage, then just before the road junction and signpost pass through a kissing-gate that flanks a wooden gate on your right.

Your well defined path passes beneath a canopy of yews, then becomes hedged as it follows the edge of the gardens to Elm Tree Farm. Beyond a small metal gate an established path keeps you to the left-hand edge of a large field and affords you good views westwards along the valley towards Odstock church. On reaching the corner of the field go through the wooden gate and bear right along a wide farm track. A line of mature trees lines the left-hand side as you proceed along the stony track towards some bungalows. Keep left when the track merges with a metalled lane, following it to the end of the properties and a sharp left-hand bend.

At this point bear off right through a gateway, then turn immediately left with the green arrow waymarking the Avon Valley Path and enter lush pasture via a metal gate. The Avon Valley Path was opened in 1992 and is a well signposted long-distance walking route, covering some 34 miles between Christchurch and Salisbury. Proceed right-handed along the edge of the field, looking out for the stile fence that is located behind a tree. The green arrow points your way straight ahead across pasture towards the large farm and Odstock village ahead. The secluded and yew shrouded St. Mary's church, the scene of gypsy revels and curses lies to your right. Keep to the right of the telegraph pole and head towards a wooden gate just beyond the barns. A line of mature beeches signifying the Avenue, an old drove route, can be seen coming off the downs towards the farm.

Climb the fence stile to the right of the gate, cross the base of the Avenue at the top of the farmyard and pass through a wooden gate, your route marked with a green arrow. A trackway leads you to a further gate, then a yellow arrow directs you along a meandering path across pasture to a fence stile. Beyond this a hedged path passes between dwellings and drops down onto a lane in the village of Odstock. Turn right along the lane and if you require refreshment the characterful thatched Yew Tree Inn has a delightful front garden in which you can relax.

At the crossroads just beyond the pub and telephone box turn left along the main village street. Oliver Cromwell is said to have stayed at the Parsonage, a 17th century house that was once an inn and located on this side of the village. Just beyond the magnificent tile-hung house called Glebe House where the lane bears round to the left, veer off right at the Avon Valley Path fingerpost and cross the stile

Walk 6

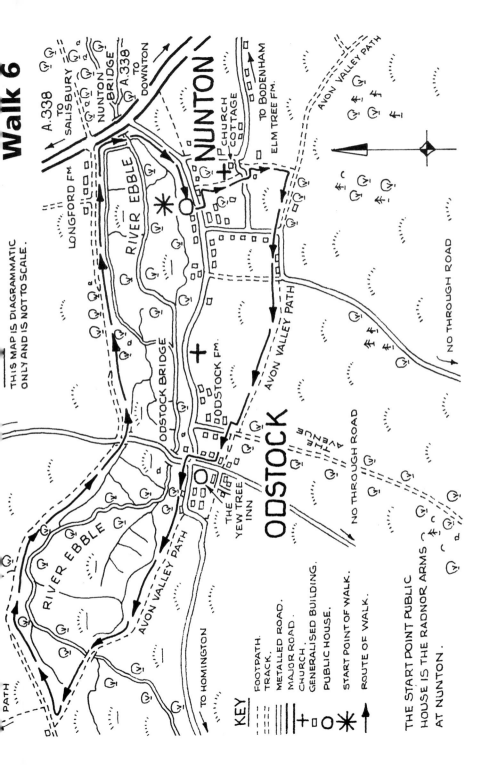

THIS MAP IS DIAGRAMMATIC ONLY AND IS NOT TO SCALE.

A.338 TO SALISBURY

NUNTON BRIDGE

A.338 TO DOWNTON

NUNTON

CHURCH COTTAGE

TO BODENHAM

ELM TREE FM.

LONGFORD FM.

RIVER EBBLE

AVON VALLEY PATH

NO THROUGH ROAD

ODSTOCK BRIDGE

ODSTOCK FM.

AVON VALLEY PATH

ODSTOCK

THE YEW TREE INN

THE AVENUE

NO THROUGH ROAD

NO THROUGH ROAD

RIVER EBBLE

AVON VALLEY PATH

TO HOMINGTON

PATH

KEY

---	FOOTPATH.
----	TRACK.
‖	METALLED ROAD.
+	MAJOR ROAD.
+	CHURCH.
□	GENERALISED BUILDING.
O	PUBLIC HOUSE.
*	START POINT OF WALK.
↑	ROUTE OF WALK.

THE START POINT PUBLIC HOUSE IS THE RADNOR ARMS AT NUNTON.

that flanks a metal gate, then keep right-handed along the wire fence across lush meadowland. Your route soon passes through a wooden gate in the fence, then almost immediately bears left through a further gate, before you head straight across the centre of pasture with downland scenes towards Odstock Down away to your left. Shortly, cross over a shallow grassy gully, which may be in flow after prolonged rain, the crystal clear water of the River Ebble soon coming into view.

Climb the stile at the end of the wire fence on the bank of the swiftly flowing chalkstream, then follow the narrow earth path through scrub and along the meandering riverbank. Disregard the stile into pasture on your right and proceed to a wooden footbridge over the river. It was here that we disturbed two herons fishing in the clear shallow waters of the Ebble. They lumbered away in silent flight in search of a quieter lunch spot on the river bank.

We lingered awhile absorbing the pastoral beauty that surrounded us before leaving the footbridge and turning immediately left across a narrow plank bridge with a wooden hand-rail. From here keep left along the river bank to an overgrown stile flanking a field entrance, which was devoid of its barbed wire fencing when we passed through it. Once in the next meadow gradually bear slightly right away from the river and cross what can be rather boggy pasture to a stile beside a wire-strung gateway. Waymarker arrows point you right along a wide grassy trackway which is lined with hedges on both sides. Ignore the Avon Valley footpath signs directing you left across a stile and proceed ahead along this delightful thorough-fare that tracks the edge of the valley, with the lines of old pollarded willows marking the meandering course of the Ebble away to your right.

When you reach the end of this wide trackway keep left to follow a well worn footpath along the right-hand edge of open farmland. Bear left as you near the field corner to follow the bridleway through a small gateway, then turn right along a grassy track which leads you right-handed along the edge of a field. Odstock Hospital can be seen up on the down away to your left. Maintain your course along what soon becomes an established grassy track and shortly reach a metalled lane. Turn right, then in a little way pass through the metal gate on your left, the blue bridleway marker indicating the right of way along what was a severely churned up muddy track. Beyond a wooden gate your route becomes more even underfoot as it follows a fine fenced grassy pathway to a further wooden gate.

A wide earth bridleway now leads you through a hazel coppice, then merges with a grass-centred farm track, shortly to pass a pair of cottages and a little further on the complex of barns and elegant farmhouse of Longford Farm. The track soon becomes a concrete farm road and maintains an easterly direction leading you to the busy A338 Salisbury to Ringwood road. Immediately opposite you is one of the gates that leads to the magnificent Longford Castle and park that borders the River Avon. Our route heads south along the footway beside the extremely noisy main road, crossing Nunton Bridge over the River Ebble before turning right along the lane towards Nunton. Leave the A338 and follow the lane into the village bearing right back to the Radnor Arms.

Footpaths and woodland ways from Rockbourne

WALK 7
Allow 3 hours
5 miles
Walk begins page 43

Background to the Walk

'The village street in Rockbourne', says Pevsner, 'is one of the prettiest in Hampshire'. This is certainly true, for the one long gently winding street in this peaceful and sheltered village, tucked in the downs between Wiltshire and Dorset, is lined with Tudor and Georgian houses and splendid thatched and timber-framed cottages. Several of the cottages, including Cruck Cottage, Glebe Cottage and Penny's Cottage are of cruck construction and those dwellings on the north side of the street are reached via little bridges that span a tiny winterbourne, known as Sweatfords Water and which flows into the River Avon. Most of the houses in the village were in Wiltshire before the revision of the county boundaries in 1895.

Pre-dating the notion of counties altogether is the church of St. Andrew, originally Norman but later changed and extended in the 13th and late-19th centuries. Located on a grassy knoll it has a tiny oak shingled spire which dates from 1630 and an ornate porch added in 1893. The interior of the church houses some interesting memorials to the Coote family who resided in West Park to the south of the village, a large house that was demolished in 1945. A memorial and portrait to General Sir Eyre Coote are situated by the organ. He was the most famous, distinguishing himself as one of Clive of India's officers at the Battle of Plessey, in Bengal, in 1757 and died in 1783. The Eyre Coote Monument, a one hundred foot pillar was erected in West Park by the East India Company in 1828 to commemorate him. It is clearly visible on the early part of this walk.

Maps
Landranger 1:50,000
Sheet 184
Pathfinder 1:25,000
Sheet SU 01/11
Map Reference of Start/
Finish SU114183.

How to get there
Rockbourne is situated 9 miles south of Salisbury. To reach the village from Salisbury head south to join A354 for Blandford Forum. Pass through Coombe Bissett, then at the top of Coombe Bissett Down bear off left onto an unclassified lane signposted Rockbourne and Roman villa. From Andover take A3057 towards Romsey, shortly to head westwards along A303. In 1 mile bear off left to join A343 for Salisbury, merge with the A30 and enter Salisbury. Follow 'through traffic' signs to pick up A354 Blandford road. There is, at present, no bus service to Rockbourne or Whitsbury from Salisbury, but please check with local operators for new service information.

Pub facilities
Rose and Thistle,
Rockbourne (right)
The idyllic appearance of the
village is maintained in this
splendid country inn, a 17th
century two-storey white-
washed building which exudes
character and style and offers
excellent food. Originally two
cottages, the Rose and Thistle
became an inn about 180 years
ago and until recently was
owned by Whitbread. After a
period of closure during 1991
a consortium of local people
decided to buy the inn. The
low beamed interior is
delightfully unspoilt and
tastefully furnished with
polished oak tables and chairs,
carved benches and cushioned
settles. Country-style fabrics,
quality prints and colourful
dried flower arrangements
enhance the civilised
atmosphere that prevails here.
The intimate lounge/dining
room has a huge inglenook
fireplace with warming log
fire, while the simpler public
bar has a flagged floor and
open stone fireplace. The bar
opens from 1100-1500 and
1800-2300 (from 1700 and all
day on Saturdays in summer
months) offering three real
ales - Wadworth 6X,
Marstons Pedigree and
Courage Best - and a good
choice of carefully chosen
wines. Bar food here is first-
class and imaginatively
presented, both the short
lunchtime snack menu and
evening selection of dishes are
home-made, using fresh
ingredients. At lunchtimes
chicken liver pate, spicy
avocado pear, ploughmans, hot
garlic and scrambled eggs
with prawns and smoked
salmon are supplemented with
a range of daily blackboard

Just below the church is Manor Farm which has a complex of medieval buildings, including a 13th century chapel and a small 14th century house to which is attached an Elizabethan east wing. An adjacent mighty 15th century barn has two magnificent waggon porches. The Manor was owned by the Cooper family during the 17th century and Ashley-Cooper, the son of Sir John Cooper was first Earl of Shaftesbury in 1672.

The oldest homestead in the village is the large Roman villa, discovered south of the village by a farmer out ferreting in 1942. Subsequent digging and excavation during the 1950s revealed that the villa had nearly 50 rooms, and a treasure house of Roman remains were uncovered, including a floor mosaic, coins, pottery, jewellery and elaborate ironwork. The villa and museum are open from Easter to September.

The neighbouring village of Whitsbury, like Rockbourne, enjoys a tranquil existence tucked away in downland. In former days however this area may well have seen some battles, for high above the northern end of the village, at a height of 400 ft. is a fine example of a fortified Iron Age camp. Whitsbury Castle covers about 16 acres and is surrounded by a triple circle of great banks with two deep ditches. It was from here that native Britons probably engaged the Saxons in battle at nearby Charford, holding them at the River Avon for over fifty years. The Castle Ditches formed part of a group of fortifications, with Clearbury Ring

Left: Whitsbury church

specials, such as a freshly
prepared soup, egg and bacon
pie, tagliatelle carbonara,
chilli, 'elegant' Welsh rarebit
or pan-fried fillets of lemon
sole. A three-course lunch is
available on Sundays. The
monthly-changing evening
menu features more elaborate
fare — escalope of veal with
mushrooms, cream and
masala, roast breast of duck in
rhubarb and brandy sauce and
good puddings like peanut
cream pie. Food is served from
1200-1400 and 1900-2200.
Children are welcome in the
small restaurant area and the
attractive front garden has a
collection of tables and
thatched dovecote. Dogs are
welcome in the bar side only.

and Old Sarum, which guarded these lonely uplands against the advancing Saxons.

Evidence of earlier habitation within the castle and village area have been found in the form of foundations of a Roman building, containing a hypocaust, together with New Forest pottery of the 2nd and 3rd century AD. These were found in a field between the church and Glebe House. Roman coins were unearthed near the castle during the last century, substantiating the fact of a Romano-British settlement here in the 2nd century.

The church of St. Leonard's stands on a steep knoll above the village and offers far-reaching views, especially south westwards, from the peaceful churchyard. The present building dates from 1878, although it is known that a church has existed here since the 12th century. It is a simple church with an odd looking brick tower and a barrel-vaulted nave.

Dominating village life and the surrounding land is Whitsbury Manor Stud, a most successful horse breeding, training and racing stables. Numerous paddocks encircle the village and the many wide tracks across the open downland nearby make ideal gallops for potential race winners. The most famous race horses that have been bred and trained here are Desert Orchid and Rhyme and Reason.

Walk 7

Distance: *Allow up to 3 hours for this five mile walk.*

Parking is limited behind the Rose and Thistle and although you are welcome to park there, it is advisable at busy times to park your vehicle behind the village hall, a short distance along the village street. From the inn bear right along the main street and in a little way turn left along a track, waymarked to the church. It is well worth strolling the length of this gently winding street, to admire this pretty village scene of elegant houses and thatched cottages that line the little chalkstream.

Return to the track and head towards the church, passing the plain Georgian vicarage, then at the wall to Manor Farm turn right with the sign pointing you to the church. At the end of a track bear left across a gravel drive towards the farmhouse and walk up a stepped path to the left of a mature topiary hedge to St. Andrew's church. The churchyard affords good downland views and overlooks Manor Farm, complete with medieval barns, houses and C13th chapel.

Proceed along the narrow grass path alongside the topiary hedge, then keep left beside a brick wall to a three-fingered footpath post. Your route continues straight on along a narrow path that tracks the rear gardens of the houses in the village. Disregard the two paths arrowed right into the village. When you reach a stile, cross over and turn immediately right over another stile, then bear half-left across pasture to a stile in the left-hand corner. Climb a further two stiles, pass to the right of a static caravan and small yard and keep right-handed along the line of telegraph poles on a worn path through pasture. The 100 foot Eyre Coote Monument is visible above the trees on the hill away to your right.

Beyond the stile in the right-hand corner of the field, turn right over another stile into lush river meadow and keep left-handed along the pasture edge towards two cottages. A yellow arrow on the next stile waymarks your path in front of a pink-washed cottage, then you drop down onto the drive of Marsh Farm before turning left and promptly right with the footpath arrow through a small wooden gate. Keep left-handed across a lawned garden to a further wooden gate, then bear half-right with the arrow to a small gate in the pasture corner. A defined pathway now leads you right-handed along the edge of a cultivated field towards a thatched cottage. Eventually, pass the cottage and reach a lane.

A short diversion can be made here if you wish to visit the Roman villa by turning right and following the lane across the brook to a T-junction, the villa entrance lies almost opposite. Our main route continues over the lane to follow a wide grass centred track, that soon becomes hedged, its edge lined with primroses on the bright early spring day when we walked this way. When you enter a small copse and reach a crossroads of tracks, bear left up a steep bank on a well worn path and pass a disused stile to emerge out onto open grassland. Turn left and head uphill, keeping to the right of a copse and shortly pass through a red metal gate. A red sign notified us that a bull is generally kept in the pasture beyond, but there was no trace if him that day. A well defined track along the edge of the field brings you to another gate, the stile to its side overgrown with brambles and disused.

You now turn right along a farm track for a short distance to where a fingerpost waymarks you left along a narrow path that follows edge of woodland downhill. On nearing a metalled drive, keep left on the main path over a small bank and remain on the well established path that passes to left of a house and garden to a metalled lane. Turn right, then almost immediately turn left at a fingerpost and enter woodland. A good worn track leads you gradually uphill through what is, in May, a glorious bluebell wood. Forestry work was under way at the time we passed through, resulting in muddy vehicle tracks and numerous side tracks.

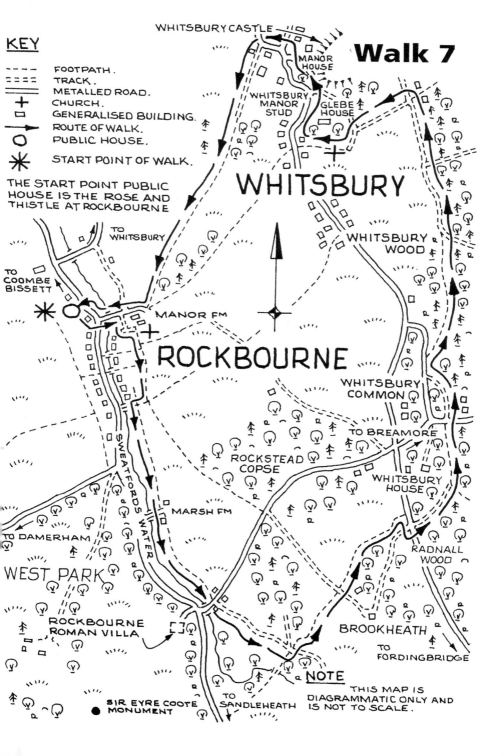

KEY

- - - - FOOTPATH.
==== TRACK.
═══ METALLED ROAD.
✝ CHURCH.
▫ GENERALISED BUILDING.
⟶ ROUTE OF WALK.
○ PUBLIC HOUSE.
✳ START POINT OF WALK.

THE START POINT PUBLIC
HOUSE IS THE ROSE AND
THISTLE AT ROCKBOURNE

Walk 7

WHITSBURY CASTLE

MANOR HOUSE

WHITSBURY MANOR STUD

GLEBE HOUSE

WHITSBURY

TO WHITSBURY

WHITSBURY WOOD

TO COOMBE BISSETT

MANOR FM

ROCKBOURNE

WHITSBURY COMMON

TO BREAMORE

ROCKSTEAD COPSE

WHITSBURY HOUSE

SWEATFORDS WATER

MARSH FM

TO DAMERHAM

WEST PARK

RADNALL WOOD

BROOKHEATH

TO FORDINGBRIDGE

ROCKBOURNE ROMAN VILLA

SIR EYRE COOTE MONUMENT

TO SANDLEHEATH

<u>NOTE</u>

THIS MAP IS
DIAGRAMMATIC ONLY AND
IS NOT TO SCALE.

Keep to the main track which soon nears the woodland edge, then at a junction of paths bear left, your route passing to the right of a large property before reaching a quiet lane.

Here you turn left, then right along a wide waymarked trackway between dwellings, then on reaching a garage bear half-left to follow the defined track which soon merges with a lane at Whitsbury Common. Briefly turn right only to veer off right again onto a delightful path that is edged with bracken and scrub to your left and woodland on your right. Pass between two large concrete bollards and venture a little to your left and pause for awhile to savour the serene rural cameo views that can be glimpsed westwards from this high woodland ridge.

Return to the main path which soon enters the peaceful realms of Whitsbury Wood, then where this enjoyable thoroughfare diverges with a track from your right proceed ahead, the woodland around you clearly marked 'private'. Shortly, you will leave the woodland to follow its edge for a few hundred yards with large horse paddocks to your left. When you reach a metalled drive and a bungalow on your right turn left to follow a grassy path between two paddocks and head towards Whitsbury church. At a T-junction of paths turn left around the church-yard to enter it via a little gate on your right. Whitsbury churchyard affords splendid views across the Avon valley towards the New Forest from its secluded hilltop position. On leaving the church follow the path ahead, pass through a small wooden gate, then walk downhill on the narrow path with Glebe House — the former rectory and only listed building in the village — away to your right.

Join the village next to the post box and tiny thatched post office and turn right to follow the lane uphill, shortly to pass the entrance to the stables of Whitsbury Manor Stud which is famed for breeding some of the best race horses in the country. Gently climb uphill, parts of Whitsbury Castle's ramparts will soon become visible in the woodland to your right, prior to passing the entrance to the Stud. Disregard the waymarked path right here, instead follow the lane left for a little way before bearing left with the footpath fingerpost where the lane veers right. Pass through two gates, then with stables and training areas to your left, follow a wide gallop south westwards with fine Wiltshire views to your right.

When you reach the end of this wide thoroughfare, keep left where it narrows and pass through a small iron gate, then follow the fenced grass path to a small wooden gate. Beyond this your route heads downhill through a line of beech and chestnut trees that flank a small coniferous plantation. At the end of the trees go through a further metal gate, then through a larger one just ahead and strike out across pasture towards Rockbourne church and Manor Farm now visible in the valley ahead. Eventually you will arrive at a farm track, bear right and cross the cattle grid into the farmyard. Keep right around the barns, pass through a gate, then with the medieval buildings of Manor Farm on view to your left, follow the track back to the main village street and turn right back to the Rose and Thistle.

Woodland tracks
and hilltop byeways
near West Dean

WALK 8
Up to 4 hours
6 ½ miles
Walk begins page 49

Background to the Walk

The charming and attractive village of West Dean lies in the valley of the River Dun and straddles the Wiltshire/Hampshire border. The Red Lion in the village centre is actually split by the boundary, a fact indicated by the county names on either side of the brick facade. In days past when opening times varied between counties and the pub had a bar in each county, there must have been some interesting discussions on when the pub actually closed! Pubs on county borders often have tall tales to tell of altercations between customers where a punch is thrown in one county but the damage done in the next and hinge on which constabulary is empowered to investigate the 'crime'. Even today the Red Lion must cause the authorities a problem or two, especially in deciding who collects the business rates!

The Red Lion forms part of the idyllic village scene that has been lost from many a rural community in England over the last fifty years or so — the traditional core. The pub overlooks the River Dun, which at this point seems to linger awhile creating effectively a village pond with wide grassy banks, a footbridge and numerous resident dabbling ducks. Heavily thatched timber-framed cottages fringe the lane opposite and complete the tranquil village picture, a scene that can be savoured with a cool drink whilst sitting on the front terrace of the pub on a warm summer's evening.

The only disturbance within the village is the Romsey to Salisbury railway which runs through the heart of the village, to the north of the Red Lion. West Dean and the neighbouring community is one of the lucky ones in the area, for they are still served by a station.

Maps
Landranger 1:50,000
Sheet 184
Pathfinder 1:25,000
Sheet SU 22/32
Map Reference of Start/
Finish SU258270

How to get there
West Dean lies nearly 8 miles east of Salisbury. From Salisbury head south east on A36 towards Southampton, the dual carriageway stretch bypassing Alderbury and Whaddon. Turn left off A36 for The Grimsteads at Whaddon and follow unclassified lanes through West Grimstead for West Dean. From Andover town centre take A3057 south for Stockbridge and Romsey, then join A303 and head westwards. At next junction take A343 south for Salisbury, passing through Middle Wallop, then just beyond junction with A30 turn left for East Winterslow. Follow unclassified lane to T-junction, turn left and head south for West Dean. Hampshire Bus service 76 from Andover to Salisbury links with Buddens Skyline Coaches service 36 to Romsey which passes through West Dean daily Monday to Saturday. Rail connections between Andover and

Salisbury are good and frequent early morning and late afternoon services between Salisbury and Romsey stop at West Dean.

Pub facilities
Red Lion
A warm summer's evening and a pint of ale could not be enjoyed better than at one of the tables on the sheltered grassy bank of the stream that fronts the Red Lion. On cooler days, the neatly refurbished interior of this listed brick-built pub offers a genuine warm welcome to all who enter. The open-plan front bar has two fireplaces, one has a warming fire, the other being purely decorative. A smaller second bar houses the bar billiards table. Three real ales are kept on draught with Flowers Original and Wadworth 6X being the regular ales, plus one constantly changing beer which is usually an unusual ale from one of the smaller breweries. The pub is open in the winter months from 1200-1430 and 1900-2300, while in the summer it opens an hour earlier at both sessions, except for Saturday when the pub may be open all day. A blackboard menu displays the daily specials which may include mushroom and mustard soup, chilli, lasagne, cottage pie, steak and stout pie and generally a pasta dish. The separate printed menu offers a range of fresh sandwiches, various ploughmans and a selection of basket meals. Traditional desserts include rice pudding, bread and butter pudding and possibly lemon cheesecake. Sunday roasts are proving very popular as are the regular

The Red Lion at West Dean

It is to the north of the railway line that the historical importance of the village can be explored. This tiny village was once a large Roman farming estate a thousand years before Salisbury Cathedral was built. Evidence of Roman occupation has been found in the excavation of three Roman villas within the parish and other villas are known to have existed at East Grimstead and Farley nearby. The site of one of the villas lies just north of the railway.

Further up the lane, hidden in the trees is a castle mound complete with a surrounding dry moat. At the time of the Domesday Book it was a manor occupied by a man called Waleran, who was the Ranger of the New Forest and the owner of several manors throughout Wiltshire at that time. Waleran is also thought to have built the notable brick tithe barn, which can be seen at Church Farm. It officially dates from the early 14th century and was part of the estate of Mottisfont Priory, ten miles away in Hampshire. It is 170 feet in length, with heavy timbers and 13 bays and once sheltered deer from the New Forest.

Close-by, and also tucked within a wood is the Borbach Chantry which was thankfully preserved as a mortuary chapel when the attached church of St. Mary was demolished. It is the oldest building in West Dean, built by Robert de Borbach in 1333 and contains a remarkable collection of memorials to the diarist John Evelyn and his family and the Pierreponts who both resided at West Dean House (now demolished) during the 1600s. One particular tomb, with wooden doors, shields a life-size statue of Robert Pierrepont, Earl of Kingston, who married one of Evelyns' eight daughters. The new church of St. Mary was built nearby in 1866 and is constructed of red brick and flint with clay tiles and a wooden belfry.

summer barbecues. Bar food is served from 1200-1400 and 1900-2200 seven days a week. Children are welcome inside and there is plenty of space for youngsters to amuse themselves outside. The large listed barn to the side of the pub is available for functions and those wishing to camp have the use of a five-acre field.

Prior to the railway wending its way along the valley bottom, transporting goods to Salisbury, there was an attempt to complete a canal navigation between Southampton and Salisbury. It was begun in 1795, but was fraught with problems from the outset, such as flooding, poor workmanship and above all lack of money. The furthest it reached was Alderbury and it was only briefly used by traffic until 1808 when it fell into decline. A canal wharf is visible in the village and the old route is crossed on our walk near East Grimstead church.

The Hampshire side of West Dean is characterised by modern day intrusions such as a large sawmill and timber-yard and the presence of the Royal Naval Armaments Depot. The depot shrouds much of the hillside between East and West Dean and is well fenced and guarded.

Walk 8

Distance: *Allow up to four hours for this six-and-a-half mile walk.*

Taking your leave from the peaceful and picturesque village scene of homely inn, babbling brook and a green fringed with heavy thatch, walk to the car park entrance and keep right along the lane to the railway crossing. Take care crossing the Romsey to Salisbury line, then almost immediately bear off left past King Georges Hall following the waymarked footpath along a metalled track. If wishing to visit the church of St. Mary and the Borbach Chantry remain on the lane for a short distance uphill.

Where the track forks, keep left to follow the driveway towards the complex of buildings known as Church Farm, part of which includes the notable 14th century brick tithe barn. Just before you reach the main gate your route bears left along a grass centred track. Look out for the stile in the wire fence on your right and cross this into pasture. Head half-left across the field, a yellow arrow on a post soon establishes your direction and a stile soon becomes visible in the gap in the wide hedge in front of you. Pass over a small brook, then climb the stile which flanks a field entrance strung with barbed wire. Proceed diagonally right across the field towards a clump of brambles at the head of a small river gully and cross the narrow plank bridge, over what can be a significant flow of water after prolonged periods of rain. You now keep right to a stile in the hedgerow.

Once in the pasture beyond the stile bear half-left and head gently uphill towards the house that is visible in the trees ahead. Soon seek out a stile that precedes woodland just to the right of the house in the corner of the field. Take a breather at the stile and absorb the view back across the very rural valley to the wooded slopes of Dean Hill. Your route now enters the woodland along a defined pathway, which shortly becomes a wide grassy path, gradually rising uphill through coppice. When you reach a plantation of tall pine trees, keep left at the fork in the path and proceed for a little way through the coniferous trees until a stile can be seen ahead on the woodland edge.

Climb the stile into a vast area of pasture that seems surrounded by woodland and belongs to Howe Farm, the large brick farmhouse that lies away to your right in the distance. Head straight across the fields which we found to be oozing with water after what had been a very wet January. Good stout walking boots were in order that day as we trudged towards the farm. Our first obstacle, close to the stile, was a small stream which we crossed via a broken tree. Luckily, the next much wider brook has a sturdy footbridge and a yellow arrow which points your way to the stile in the fence ahead. Another arrow on the stile waymarks you half-right across a paddock towards two trees and a new stile just to their left. The going underfoot may well be tough during winter months as the paddock becomes waterlogged and horses hooves create an uneven surface.

Turn right once you are over the stile, then climb another stile before turning left along the wire fence, eventually reaching a double wooden stile in the paddock fencing. Cross the paddock to another stile, then bear diagonally right across pasture to the far corner and a small wooden footbridge which leads you into the woodland fringe. The established path almost immediately bears right across scrub to an unmetalled track. Turn left and remain on this woodland track for a short distance to a junction of gravel tracks, where your route bears left and passes to the side a green metal barrier to enter Bentley Wood on a wide gravel unmetalled track.

Bentley Wood is owned by the Countryside Commission and covers an area of 170 acres. An information board beside the gravel track explains that the woodland is of particular scientific interest for its abundant wildlife. Twenty-three species of butterfly, over 400 species of moth, 100 species of birds and some 400 types of plants — including spotted orchids and meadow saffron — can be found within this peaceful woodland haven.

Proceed along this track, past the information board, then look out for a crossroads of grassy tracks (not waymarked). If you reach the point where the main track forks sharp left, you have gone too far. Having located these green thoroughfares turn right and keep to this defined wide pathway through the trees to a stile on the woodland edge. Here you join a narrow tree-lined gravel path, which had transformed itself into a miniature stream on the day we walked it, a result of the recent heavy rain. This soon becomes a metalled lane as you enter the farming hamlet of East Grimstead.

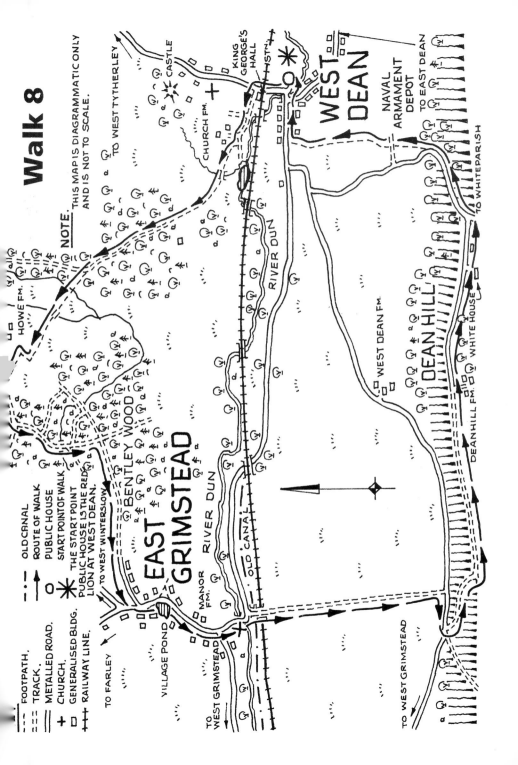

When you reach the main village lane turn left, pass the village pond and stay on this very quiet lane, heading gently downhill to the River Dun and East Grimstead's Holy Trinity church. This delightful little flint-built church was unfortunately locked when we tried the door, and there was no indication of where one could obtain the key to view its interior. At the sharp left-hand bend by the church keep ahead on a tarmac lane and cross over the course of the now very neglected Southampton to Salisbury Canal Navigation, then proceed uphill soon to cross the bridge over the railway. The lane becomes a wide hedged chalky track as it passes East Grimstead quarry to your left. Water may linger in the hollows along this track, but the grassy verges aid a dry passage as you gradually rise uphill towards the steep chalk escarpment that looms ahead.

When you arrive at what can be a busy lane, turn right and follow it for approximately 100 yards before turning sharp left onto a waymarked bridleway which climbs diagonally up the steep ridge. It is worth pausing at intervals as you ascend the chalky track for the views that begin to unfold are magnificent. Once on top, turn left at a crossroads of old thoroughfares to join a grassy track that follows the crest of the ridge.

You are now following the route of an ancient road that once linked London with Weymouth in Dorset. Most of the first highways followed the chalk ridges for they were drier and more direct. This ridge dominates the landscape for miles around and the views extend to all parts of the compass, south to the wooded area of the New Forest, north and east across open stretches of fertile farmland interspersed with copse, but most dramatic of all is to look north westwards towards the Avon Valley and pick out Salisbury's Cathedral spire, which marks the eastern confluence of five river valleys.

Shortly, the track becomes stony and tree-lined, then merges with the metalled driveway to Deanhill Farm which lies to your right. Yew and holly trees become evident as you track this ridgeway route towards Dean Hill, a sure sign that this was an old highway as these hardy trees provided good shelter from harsh northerly winds. This delightful stretch of the walk affords views across the sleepy village of West Dean, nestling in the valley below. Pass through a thick yew wood, then in front of the gates to White House and proceed to the end of this fine driveway to a lane, opposite a communications mast.

Turn left and follow this quiet lane which descends Dean Hill. Near the base of the hill at a sharp left-hand bend a fingerpost directs you right along a defined grass path beside the awesome high black fences of the Naval Armament Depot. These ugly fences encircle the vast complex of huge bomb bunkers which extend along the side of the hill, dominating West Dean from this angle. Cross a stile by the main gate and walk beside the perimeter fence to another stile. Here thankfully, you leave the fence to follow a defined path along the left-hand edge of a crop field towards the village. When you reach a house, keep left along its garden fence to a stile and drop down onto a lane, then turn right back into the village centre and the Red Lion.

Valley paths and downland ways near Broad Chalke

WALK 9
At least 3 hours
6 miles
Walk begins page 55

Background to the Walk

The Ebble Valley is my favourite of all the valleys that radiate out from the city of Salisbury. The thirteen mile long chalk stream — known as the Ebble or Chalkebourne — begins its life at the base of the rolling chalk downland of Cranborne Chase and flows eastwards through a totally unspoilt and peaceful sheltered valley, merging with the River Avon just south of the city. Time seems to have passed the valley and its string of tranquil villages by, for it is free from the humdrum and pace of busy main roads and the associated developments that spring up along their corridors. Narrow lanes linked the numerous isolated farmsteads, hamlets and small villages, which lay hidden in the folds of the chalk hills that protect the valley to the north and south.

The largest of these villages is Broad Chalke, which lies where the main valley road meets the lanes from Bowerchalke and the narrow route from Martin and Damerham, and has developed on both sides of the River Ebble, with a causeway bridge linking the two. The heart of the village clusters to the south of the river, away from the main valley road, and comprises some fine examples of stone, cob and timber-framed thatched cottages as well as some fine large and imposing brick houses. The latter residences are said to have been built as winter homes for the farmers from nearby Cranborne Chase, who retreated here in search of some social life during the long cold months. Of particular note is the early 18th century brick manor house called Reddish Manor and the attractive stone-built Kings Old Rectory with its brick chimney and mullioned windows.

Maps
Landranger 1:50,000
Sheet 184
Pathfinder 1:25,000
Sheet SU 02/12
Map Reference of Start/
Finish SU039256

How to get there
Broad Chalke lies 8 miles south west of Salisbury. From the city centre head south following signs for Blandford and Weymouth to join A354. After 3 miles in Combe Bissett, turn right for Bishopstone to follow the valley bottom road for five miles into Broad Chalke. The Queens Head is located on this road. From Andover follow A3057 south for Romsey and Stockbridge, then head west along A303 for 1 mile before joining A343 signed to Salisbury. Merge with A30 and continue into the city, following 'through traffic' signs south to join A354 Blandford road. Wilts and Dorset Bus service 29 between Salisbury and Shaftesbury via the Chalke Valley stops in Broadchalke. Wilts and Dorset/Hampshire Bus services 7, 8, 9 and Hampshire Bus services 76/76A link Andover with Salisbury as does the railway.

Pub facilities
Queen's Head
(Pictured right)
This lovely 15th century flint building was once the village bakehouse and stables before becoming an inn. The main Village bar has a warm and friendly atmosphere with part exposed brick and flint walls, lots of black painted beams and a huge inglenook with open log fire. Furnishings are traditional with a mixture of pub tables and chairs and wall bench seating. There is an adjacent restaurant/function room. The bar opens from 1200-1500 and 1900-2300, with the usual hours on Sundays and serves four real ales — Wadworth 6X, Hook Norton Best Bitter, Ringwood Best Bitter and Bass — and a good selection of country wines from its well stocked bar. Traditional style bar food can be ordered between 1200-1400 and 1900-2115, from a short blackboard menu featuring daily specials like jugged hare, braised lamb chops, savoury home-made quiche and lemon soufflé and from a comprehensive printed menu, which include such dishes as lasagne, chicken curry, casserole of beef, a choice of steaks, local trout, grilled salmon steak, ploughmans, omelettes, sandwiches and soups. Vegetarian choices include cheese and nut croquettes, nut roast Portugaise and vegetable curry. Fine weather imbibing can be enjoyed in the sheltered courtyard, across which lies the accommodation block with four comfortable double rooms. Walkers are welcome to park their cars in the car park, if permission is asked first.

The Kings Old Rectory was once the home of the 17th-century diarist John Aubrey, who was also a fine historian, particularly concerning his native county of Wiltshire. He wrote affectionately of the village and its river — 'There are no better trouts in the Kingdom of England than here' — and the surrounding country-side with its gentle slopes and avenues of trees. Aubrey became church-warden and helped to restore the then derelict All Saints church, which dates from the 13th century. Its large cruciform shape stands on foundations older than itself and its 15th century central tower rests on an imposing group of pointed arches. Inside, there are two fine roofs, one old and one new. The old one is the trussed rafter roof in the north transept; the other covers the nave, and though new, rests on beautiful old corbels carved with angels playing musical instruments. There are six bells in the tower, the last having been added by the church-wardens George Penruddocke and John Aubrey, the latter describing them as 'one of the tunablest ring of bells in Wiltshire'.

Over the past century the important industry of watercress production has flourished around the village, due to presence of numerous springs that bubble up from the chalk strata on its western fringe. The crystal clear water is of a constant temperature and flows all year round, enabling the industry to survive in an area where fluctuating water levels, or drying up of springs, have resulted in the demise of watercress production elsewhere in the county.

Font in Broad Chalke church

The early stages of your walk tracks the River Ebble as it heads eastwards and explores the lush valley bottom farmland as you make your way to the straggling village of Bishopstone. The village has developed from the growing together of several farming settlements, such as Croucheston, Faulston, Netton, Flamston, The Pitts and Throope, all of which have retained their old names. The name — Bishopstone — derives from the time when the Bishop of Winchester once owned the manor and it was probably this episcopal influence that ensured the survival of its name to this day, for in many cases such village names were demoted to street or area names.

At one of the farmsteads — Faulston — can be found a magnificent Dovecote and other buildings of architectural and historical interest. The large, round dovecote is thought to be of pre-Reformation age and is built of flint and stone in bands, topped with a conical tiled roof. Faulston House dates from the late 17th century and is surrounded by a flint-stone wall, which indicates that it once surrounded an earlier building.

Also worth seeking out, although not on our route, is the tiny hamlet of Fifield Bavant which lies about a mile west of Broad Chalke. St. Martins church is one of the smallest churches in England, 35 feet long and 15 feet wide, and is perched alone in a field on top of a grassy hill that overlooks the meadows where the former village was situated. The church contains a Norman font and the roof beams are dark with age. The name of the hamlet is said to derive from five fields or hides of land, hence Fifield and Bavant comes from the name of the Norman owners.

Walk 9

Distance: *Allow up to three hours for this walk of six miles.*

From the inn cross the lane and follow the lane opposite, which is signed to Bowerchalke, towards the church. In a little way pass over the causeway bridge that spans the crystal clear waters of the Ebble, then bear right through the church car park to enter All Saints churchyard. It is well worth perusing the historical notes in the church for a few minutes before making for the lych-gate at the end of the path. Away to your right you will see the grave of Sir Cecil Beaton who died in 1980. Once on the village lane, turn left and enjoy a short stroll into the heart of the village to view the assortment of attractive cottages and the fine large properties called Reddish Manor and Kings Old Rectory.

Return to the lych-gate, then follow the lane left round the churchyard, its bank covered in primroses on spring days. Just beyond the bungalow on your right, lookout for a yellow arrow waymarking your route right along the edge of its garden. Pass beside the garage, climb two stiles, then keep left-handed along the edge of pasture, shortly to leave the fence to follow a line of trees and later a hedge to a stile in the field corner. The peaceful meandering channel of the Ebble lies to your left and unspoilt rural scenes greet the eye, whichever way you look.

Cross the stile and pass through a small clump of trees to a lane. Turn left, heading towards the river bridge, then turn right to join an arrowed path which follows the left-hand edge of a vast open field, with the Ebble babbling away just beyond the trees on your left. Maintain your course towards the buildings ahead and eventually drop down off the field, by the river's edge to a stile, then bear right along the driveway to Knighton Mill. Pass between the beautifully converted mill house and a large black barn, your track soon bearing left away from another vast barn to join a metalled lane. Keep left and soon pass on your right Knighton Manor Farm, which has a fine 16th century doorway.

Where the lane veers sharp right towards a bungalow, proceed straight ahead onto a grass-centred trackway, disregarding the green waymarker arrowing a path right, following the track to a large pair of metal gates and a large crop field beyond. If the field is in crop, bear left and follow the perimeter fence, otherwise strike out across the field, heading towards the far left-hand corner. To your left, the pretty thatched cottages in the isolated hamlet of Stoke Farthing can be seen nestling close to the banks of the river. Older still, and visible on your right is a medieval field system of strip lynchets, which are furrowed into the steep scarp slope of Knighton Hill. Keep your eyes peeled, for you are likely to see a few hares as you make your way across this open field.

In the far corner, pass through two rusty old iron gates and soon join a defined track that takes you past Croucheston Mill, one of two mills that the River Ebble once powered. Croucheston Mill produces animal feedstuffs and belongs to Mole Valley Feeds. Lower Mill close by, once had a water wheel which powered 19th century machinery and ground corn before it became a private house during the Second World War. Beyond the mill, at a metalled lane, bear right to pass Fieldgrove House and follow the lane into Croucheston, one of the many old farming settlements that make up the scattered community of Bishopstone.

Remain on this lane to where it bears left past Cheriton House and turn right to follow a tarmac lane in a southerly direction. This shortly gives way to a stony earth track just beyond a brick thatched cottage, called Drove Cottage. This name reveals a great deal about the history of this area, for the valley and high chalk downs are criss-crossed with numerous wide hedged hollow lanes. The signifi-

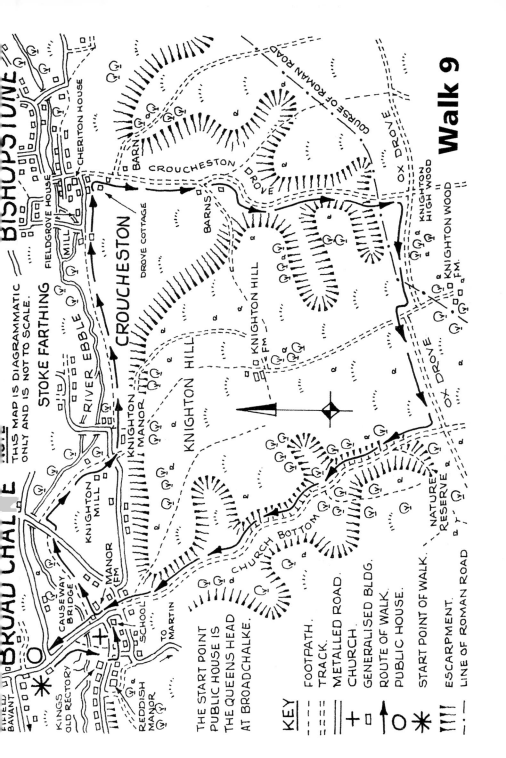

Walk 9

THIS MAP IS DIAGRAMMATIC ONLY AND IS NOT TO SCALE.

BISHOPSTONE

BROAD CHALKE

STOKE FARTHING

CROUCHESTON

CROUCHESTON DROVE

COURSE OF ROMAN ROAD

OX DROVE

KNIGHTON HIGH WOOD

KNIGHTON WOOD

KNIGHTON FM.

OX DROVE

KNIGHTON HILL FM.

KNIGHTON HILL

KNIGHTON MANOR

RIVER EBBLE

FIELDGROVE HOUSE

MILL

CHERITON HOUSE

BARN

DROVE COTTAGE

BARNS

KNIGHTON MILL

MANOR FM.

CAUSEWAY BRIDGE

SCHOOL

TO MARTIN

CHURCH BOTTOM

NATURE RESERVE

KINGS OLD RECTORY

REDDISH MANOR

FIFIELD BAVANT

THE START POINT PUBLIC HOUSE IS THE QUEENS HEAD AT BROADCHALKE.

KEY

- - -	FOOTPATH.
= = =	TRACK.
═══	METALLED ROAD.
+ ◻	CHURCH.
◻	GENERALISED BLDG.
↑○	ROUTE OF WALK.
○	START POINT OF WALK.
✳	PUBLIC HOUSE.
∥∥∥	ESCARPMENT.
— · —	LINE OF ROMAN ROAD

cant routes are the ancient hill-top drove-ways on either side of the Ebble Valley. To the north, the Salisbury Way linked Salisbury to Shaftesbury and the west country, while on the southern ridge the Ox Drove provided a route into Dorset and linked up with the Roman Road from Old Sarum to Dorchester. The importance of these routes in the earliest of days can be traced through the presence of tumulli, earthworks and barrows dotted across the downland.

Your route from here follows Croucheston Drove, a defined hedged trackway that linked the valley farmsteads to the main east to west green ways. One can imagine the scenes of days past, when fattened sheep were driven from the shelter of the lush valleys up onto the high and dry chalk ridges, to begin their long journey to market. Today, these tracks provide tractor access to fields and perfect rambling by-ways for the walker wishing to escape into this tranquil landscape. In a little way pass through a metal gate, with barns to your left and begin to gradually ascend the downland mass in front of you. Pass another barn on your right and the track — Bishopstone Hollow — then remain on this fine hedged hollow lane as it winds its way through a deep dry chalk valley, before climbing sharply up the main scarp slope.

At the top, catch your breath and savour the view that has revealed itself back down the snaking dry valley into the Ebble Valley and across the rolling expanse of farmland that top the downland. When you reach a T-junction of tracks, turn right onto the ancient Ox Drove and head westwards. Peek through the hedge to your left for good views south into Dorset and Hampshire. The track skirts the edge of Kington High Wood and soon crosses the route of the old Roman Road (not visible) between Old Sarum to Dorchester.

At a metalled road, which leads to Kington Wood Farm, tucked in the woodland to your left, turn right for a short distance to where the Ox Drove resumes its course westwards. At a crossroads of tracks, turn right and begin your descent off this exposed chalk ridge track back down into the Ebble Valley. The wide established chalk holloway descends into a delightful dry valley, known as Church Bottom. Near the top a Wiltshire Trust Nature Reserve sign on your left, indicates that access to the land is permitted and it is worth exploring, especially in early summer when there is a splendid display of characteristic chalk downland flowers.

Follow the trackway for three quarters of a mile down through Church Bottom and its rich sheep grazing pasture, towards Broad Chalke church, eventually passing a large house on your left before reaching a crossroads. Go straight on, head for the church, then at the road junction opposite the church bear right to rejoin the lane that leads you back across the river to the Queens Head and your transport.

Nadder Valley paths and villages from Chicksgrove

WALK 10
At least 4 hours
7 miles
Walk begins page 61

Background to the Walk

The Nadder Valley is quite unlike any of the other river valleys that radiate out from Salisbury, for it is not a distinct deep valley incised in the chalk strata as is evident in the neighbouring Ebble and Wylye river valleys. This anomalous character is due to the fact that the Nadder traverses a sequence of rock types, resulting in a landscape of scarp slopes and deep coombs within its broad vale. In this well-watered valley, villages are free from the need to be located on the banks of the Nadder, and are found scattered across the landscape, nestling among lush meadows, wooded hills and along gentle tributary streams. This seven mile walk explores the heart of the Nadder Valley, its changing scenery and the charming unspoilt villages, encouraging the visitor to linger.

One such settlement is Chicksgrove, a collection of scattered cottages and houses that enjoy an idyllic isolated location among the folds of the hills, close to the Nadder and reached only by narrow country lanes.

Two of the most picturesque villages in the Nadder Valley — Teffont Evias and Teffont Magna — are located on the Teff stream, a tumbling little brook which gushes from the ground just north of the latter and flows through both villages into Teffont Park and the Nadder. The name Teffont comes from the Anglo-Saxon words 'teo' meaning boundary and 'funta' meaning stream.

Teffont Evias is the smaller of the two and is the most peaceful, being located along a tiny lane away from the busy B-road. It is so named Evias or Ewyas after Ewyas Harold in Herefordshire, whose barons once owned

Maps
Landranger 1:50,000
Sheet 184
Pathfinder 1:25,000
Sheets ST 82/92, SU 03/13
Map Reference of Start/
Finish ST974293

How to get there
Chicksgrove is located 1 mile off A30, approximately 11 miles west of Salisbury. From the city centre follow signs for The West A30, A303 towards Wilton and Warminster and leave Salisbury on A36. At the roundabout at Wilton turn left, pass through the town keeping straight on across the traffic lights to follow A30 for 8 miles, through Barford and Fovant, then take the third turning right — the pub is signposted. After a quarter of a mile turn left and follow this narrow lane for a further three-quarters of a mile to the Compasses Inn. From Andover head south on A3057 for Stockbridge, then join A303 and head west for 1 mile to the next junction, to follow A343 for Salisbury. Merge with A30 and proceed into Salisbury. At the first main roundabout take the fourth exit and follow signs for Warminster and The West. Wilts & Dorset Bus service 25 between Salisbury and Hindon calls at Dinton and

Teffont Magna and service 26/
27 linking Salisbury with
Hindon/Shaftesbury stop at
both Dinton and Fovant.
Wilts & Dorset/Hampshire
Bus services 7, 8, 9 and
Hampshire Bus services 76/
76A link Andover to
Salisbury as does the railway.

Pub facilities
Compasses Inn (Right)
A timeless air of peace and
tranquillity pervades within
this attractive 16th century
thatched inn, set in unspoilt
rural countryside. The long
and low beamed bar has bare
brick walls, well-worn
flagstone floors, a large
inglenook with warming
woodburner and an
assortment of traditional
furniture. Farming tools and
tackle decorate the walls. A
separate dining room/
children's room has doors
opening out to a lawned area
with benches and swings.
Four real ales — Adnams
Bitter, Bass, Wadworth 6X
and a weekly guest ale — are
served between 1200-1500 and
1800-2300 and a twice daily-
changing blackboard menu
features a short range of
excellent home-made dishes.
Fresh asparagus, country
vegetable soup, dressed crab
and smoked salmon could be
the choice of starters, followed
by steak, wine and mushroom
pie, chicken curry, macaroni
cheese, thatched vegetable pie
or cold honey glazed ham. At
lunchtimes a selection of
sandwiches and ploughmans
are also offered and on
Sundays the buffet lunch is a
popular event. Bar food served
daily, except Tuesdays, from
1230-1430 and 1900-2200.
Board games and table skittles
(cont. at top of page 61)

the manor house. The Teff stream flows beside the lane
and most of the attractive cottages are approached by
little bridges over the swiftly flowing stream. Other
houses are more imposing, the cream-coloured
Chilmark stone having been used to build a series of
mansions within spacious, stone-walled gardens and a
classic example is the beautifully proportioned
Howards House, now a private hotel.

The most imposing building in the village is the
Manor House, which with its outbuildings, cottages
and adjoining church makes one of the most striking
collections of buildings in the county. It is early 17th
century with 19th century additions and has now been
converted into flats. The church of St. Michael and All
Angels has its origins in the 12th century, the present
structure being the result of extensive repairs and
rebuilding carried out by John Mayne, Lord of the
Manor, in 1821. Its graceful, richly ornamented 125 ft
steeple was added a few years later. Of particular note
in the church is the Ley Chapel, which contains a tomb
with stone effigies of Henry Ley, a former owner of the
manor, and two of his six sons. Also note the stained
glass in the east window, installed in 1951 using ancient glass originally collected by John Mayne.

Where the lane meets the B3089, Barford to Hindon
road, the two Teffonts merge. Teffont Magna is a
charming village of thatched cottages clustering round
the medieval Church of St. Edward, where a rare
narrow-waisted bell is kept on the windowsill. On the

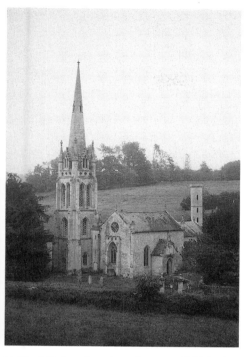

Teffont Evias church and manor (hidden).

can be played. The cobbled courtyard to the front has some seating and their are benches on the adjoining front lawn. Bed and breakfast is available. Walkers may use the car park, but arrive early at weekends as it can get busy.

jambs of the south door are scratched two medieval ships, quite unusual for an inland church. One of the most interesting houses in the village is Fitz House, a gabled building of the 17th century, once the collecting house for local wool — its fine barn still stands. Between the wars the house was occupied by the author Edith Olivier and at a later date by Sigfried Sassoon, the poet. The gardens are often open to the public.

Walk 10

Distance: *At least four hours for this seven mile walk*

Leaving the Compasses behind you turn left onto the tiny lane, following it downhill to cross the railway, then the bridge over the Nadder, before reaching a T-junction of lanes. Turn right, then in a little way your route bears off left to join a delightful tree-canopied sunken footpath, that is fringed with fragrant cow parsley and campion in late spring. Climb gently uphill, your path becoming tree-lined as it emerges from the deep cutting and levels out at the top of the rise. The path is well used as a bridleway, so it can become a little muddy especially where you pass an old pond.

Shortly, pass between two gates and remain on your narrow defined path which soon begins to descend, crossing a wide trackway, into mixed woodland. When you reach a lane, turn left, then almost immediately bear off right into the entrance to Ministry of Defence property and head for the large metal gates and level crossing over the single track railway. These gates are always locked during the day, but a bell on the left-hand gate post summons the MoD police in the nearby gatehouse, who will open the gates so that you can resume your walk.

The bridleway now heads uphill over the downland to merge with a grass-centred farm track. Keep right and follow this peaceful scenic thoroughfare for half-a-mile, then descend towards the village of Teffont Evias. Pass a group of barns, two 17th century lime kilns in the hillside on your right and two attractive thatched cottages before reaching the quiet stream-edged village lane.

It is worth lingering in this most attractive of Wiltshire villages to seek out the

Manor House and church, which lie down the lane to your right, beyond Howard House Hotel. Saunter back up the lane, passing a delightful selection of ston cottages and larger properties until you reach the busy B-road, the Black Hors and the larger sister village of Teffont Magna. Keep left along the footway and i you wish to explore the heart of the village, continue on over the rise.

Your main route crosses the B-road, just beyond the bus stop, to where footpath fingerpost, obscured in the hedge, waymarks you up the driveway t Holt View and towards the village of Dinton. Pass between two properties, the just beyond a newly built garage, bear off left between a concrete hard-standin; and coniferous trees to a small wooden gate. You now head slightly right uphi across pasture to a further wooden gate, visible on the edge of woodland. Beyon the gate, a narrow worn path leads you uphill through a beech and holly wood which has a carpet of bluebells in the spring, to a T-junction of paths. Bear righ then at a crossroads of paths, turn right again to follow the holly fringed pathway close to the woodland edge, eventually reaching a gate on its perimeter.

At this point, when we walked this way, the land ahead was being redeveloped small lakes were being dug and vast amounts of earth being moved. A Count Council Rights of Way board assured us that the path still existed and that it woul be well marked on completion of the work. Pass to the left of the gate and hea straight on along a defined grassy path, towards a small gate on the edge of th isolated copse in front of you. Pass through this rhododendron and foxglove-fille stretch of mixed deciduous woodland, looking out for deer and woodpeckers both of which we spied here. Leave the copse and head for the trees in the far right hand corner of the redeveloped land.

A National Trust sign beside a wooden gate notifies you that you are about t enter Dinton Park. A wide fence-lined path leads you to a stile, then continu ahead across parkland to a further stile, with the large mansion of Philipps Hous appearing on the hillside to your left. Climb the stile, keep right-handed round th parkland edge, which affords lovely views towards Dinton church and across th wooded Nadder Valley. On nearing the far right-hand corner of the pasture, joi a grass-centred track, that skirts the edge of a patch of unspoilt meadow and soo bear right with the track as it enters a further pasture. At this point, a worthwhil diversion is to turn left along the field edge to pick up the path that leads to Dinto church, for there is much to see in this charming village.

Back on the main route, you follow the track towards the B3089, then just prio to the road, cross a stile on your right and bear left-handed round the field edg on a waymarked path to a stile in the hedge. Cross the B-road and stile beyond then head half-right across pasture, your path is signed to Teffont Mill. Pas between telegraph poles and cross the stile in the tree-lined hedgerow ahead, ther follow the defined grassy path across a field into a narrow stretch of woodland Emerge from the trees, turn left along the edge of an arable field — if it is in crop — and make for the stile that flanks an overgrown gate, which precedes th railway. Carefully cross the track, go over the stile beyond, then bear half-righ

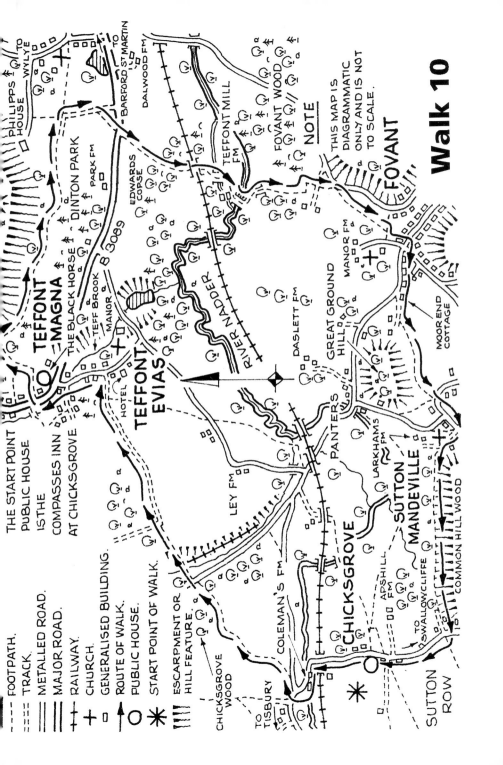

Walk 10

NOTE

THIS MAP IS DIAGRAMMATIC ONLY AND IS NOT TO SCALE.

- - - - FOOTPATH.
≡≡≡ TRACK.
═══ METALLED ROAD.
▬▬▬ MAJOR ROAD.
+-+-+ RAILWAY.
✝ CHURCH.
▫ GENERALISED BUILDING.
→ ROUTE OF WALK.
O PUBLIC HOUSE.
* START POINT OF WALK.
⋔⋔⋔ ESCARPMENT OR HILL FEATURE.

THE START POINT PUBLIC HOUSE IS THE COMPASSES INN AT CHICKSGROVE.

TEFFONT MAGNA

TEFFONT EVIAS

FOVANT

CHICKSGROVE

SUTTON MANDEVILLE

SUTTON ROW

PHILIPPS HOUSE
TO WYLYE
TO BARFORD ST MARTIN
DALWOOD FM
DINTON PARK
PARK FM
B 3089
THE BLACK HORSE
EDWARDS COPSE
TEFFONT MILL FM
FOVANT WOOD
MANOR
TEFF BROOK
HOTEL
RIVER NADDER
DASLETT FM
GREAT GROUND HILL
MANOR FM
MOOR END COTTAGE
PANTERS
LEY FM
LARKHAMS FM
COLEMAN'S FM
APSHILL FM
TO SWALLOWCLIFFE
COMMON HILL WOOD
CHICKSGROVE WOOD
TO TISBURY

through lush meadowland towards Teffont Mill, located on the River Nadder.

Your path follows the left-hand edge of the pasture, then just before the mill an stone bridge, cross a stile in the fence and go over a small wooden footbridge. Fror here you follow the yellow arrows right around a paddock, in front of the Mil' then right to a white swing gate close to the main river channel and sluice gatt Cross the river and pause to absorb the beautiful setting of the Mill, tucket peacefully in this verdant valley. Yellow arrows ensure you keep to the pat beside the river to a stile, then they direct you across a lush river meadow to footbridge over a tiny tributary stream.

Beyond the bridge, climb up a steep grassy bank to a stile, then bear half-righ to follow the thick hedgerow on your left, along the edge of pasture. When yo near the corner of the field, bear right through a metal kissing gate, then head halt left across the corner of boggy pasture to another kissing gate to join a narrov grassy path that leads you to a kissing gate and a grass centred tarmac drive. Cros this and the stile beyond and bear diagonally left with the arrow, uphill acros pasture towards the far corner of the woodland ahead. Your path cuts across th corner of the wood via two stiles, then proceeds right-handed down the tree-line mature hedgerow of a field to a stile near its far corner. You now drop down narrow path into the valley bottom to a stile, bear right to cross the brook that run through Fovant and shortly join the village lane leading to Fovant church.

Turn right if you have time to visit the 15th century church with its splendit tower. Turn left to begin the final section of your walk and follow the lane to the main village road. Turn right for Tisbury, climb gently uphill to where a footpatl fingerpost waymarks you to Sutton Mandeville, along a track in front of Moor Ent Cottage. Shortly, on reaching a driveway to a house, bear off left — ignoring th stile immediately left — to follow a defined narrow path between a hedge ant trees, eventually passing to the rear of a cottage to join its banked tarmac driveway which leads you out to a lane. Turn right and enter the hamlet of Suttor Mandeville, disregarding the lane off to your right, signed to Chilmark, then or passing a cottage called The Homestead turn right by a small green and fir tree ant head up a driveway, waymarked to the church.

Where the drive splits, keep left for Larkhams Farm, then in a little way bear of left onto a concrete path into the churchyard to All Saints church which boasts t magnificent yew tree planted in 1780 and a sundial with a ball on top, set on a stont monument dated 1685. Inside the Norman church treasures include a beautifully carved Jacobean pulpit and a 13th century chancel arch. From the porch, turn righ through the churchyard on a grassy path to a metal gate in the wall, then bear righ to follow an established path that gently descends to a wooden gate.

Climb the stile to the left of the gate, continue straight on with the arrows following the fence on your right to a stile, then proceed left-handed along the edge of a couple of fields until you join a grass-centred track, beyond an old meta gate. When you reach a lane turn right and remain on this for a quarter-of-a-mile back to the Compasses.

In and around Collingbourne Wood from Cadley

WALK 11
Allow 3 hours
5 miles
Walk begins page 67

Background to the Walk

The two Collingbourne villages lie in the Bourne Valley, a tiny intermittent flowing chalk stream that rises at Burbage to the north. For most of its length it is a winterbourne only, flowing only when the chalk becomes saturated and the springs rise in the pond at Burbage. During most of the summer months the stream bed is bone dry. Collingbourne Ducis and Kingston were once medieval forest villages, when the extensive Forest of Chute stretched out towards Savernake Forest in the north and to Salisbury in the south. The forest and its villages were important recreation and hunting grounds for royalty before it was disafforested by Charles I in 1639 and divided among favoured noble gentlemen. Today, the territory is bare and treeless with the exposed eastern fringe of Salisbury Plain and its various army activities dominating the landscape to the west of the valley. To the east, one of the last remaining areas of the ancient forest — Collingbourne Wood — shrouds the neighbouring hills.

Collingbourne Ducis derives its name from having once been held by the Duchy of Lancaster and during the 13th century it belonged to the family of William de Valence, who also held Swindon. Two settlements — Cadley and Sunton — help make up the modern day parish of Collingbourne Ducis, but for many years the valley and its village were thought to be too remote to be of any interest. It was not until the development of more efficient means of road transport that trade flourished between the villages and the markets towns of Marlborough and Andover. With the coming of the railway and the line between those two towns, a station

Maps
Landranger 1:50,000
Sheet 184
Pathfinder 1:25,000
Sheet SU 25/35
Map Reference of Start/
Finish SU254538

How to get there
Collingbourne Ducis is situated nine-and-a-half miles north west of Andover. From the town centre either follow the Ring Road west, signed Exeter A303 and Devizes A342, or head west along B3402 through the town to reach the large roundabout preceding A303. Take the exit signed Devizes A342 and Marlborough A346. Proceed through Weyhill and in three-and-a-half miles enter Ludgershall. In the town centre turn right with A342, then in a mile fork off right onto A346 towards Marlborough. Take the next turning right, signed Wexcombe and follow this unclassified lane for 1 mile to Cadley and the Shears Inn. From the Ring Road in Salisbury head north signed M3, A30 London and Andover, then at the roundabout beyond the railway bridge, take the first exit to join A338 for the Winterbournes. Remain on A338, pass beneath A303 and

*go through Shipton Bellinger
and Tidworth before reaching
Collingbourne Ducis. At the
T-junction with A346, turn
left, then in a short distance
turn right, signed Cadley to
reach the Shears Inn.
Hampshire Bus service 15
between Andover and
Swindon, via Marlborough
calls at Collingbourne Ducis.
On Saturdays Wilts & Dorset
service X19 (one bus each
way) links Salisbury to
Swindon and stops in
Collingbourne Ducis,
allowing five-and-a-half hours
between buses. From the
village it is a half mile walk to
the Shears, via the lane to
Cadley.*

Pub facilities
Shears Inn, Cadley
*This attractive brick and inn
flint was built in the 16th
century as a coaching inn. The
name derives from the fact
that sheep were sheared here
before being sold at Weyhill
market. The original building
has been extended to the rear
to provide comfortable en suite
accommodation. A comfortable
sofa and fresh flowers grace
the rear entrance lobby, off
which the modern and
spacious main bar is located.
Neatly furnished with
darkwood tables and chairs,
the odd carved oak bench and
one or two pieces of old
furniture, it is a pleasant to
relax with a pint of ale —
Foxley's Bitter and Hook
Norton Best — and to enjoy
some good value bar food. A
twice-daily changing menu
may feature a home-made
tomato and spring onion soup,
chicken, ham & mushroom
pie, steak and kidney pie,
cheese and bacon quiche, game
pate, ploughmans, salads and*

was built in the village, which encouraged the parish to grow and incorporate neighbouring settlements. The railway was dismantled during the Beeching era in the 1960s.

The village is now spread out along the A346 and contains a varied range of buildings, from modern council housing to interesting old timbered and thatched properties, that can be found beside the Bourne stream at Sunton. In particular, the brick and flint built Sunton Cottage has a deep overhanging thatch that almost touches the ground, and at nearby Church Farm there can be seen a long thatched and black weatherboarded barn. The oldest foundations in the village however, belong to St. Andrew's church. It is believed that at the time of the Domesday Book, the original church was already in ruins. It was rebuilt in the twelfth and thirteenth centuries and restored in 1876-77. Inside, there are tombs of the Seymour family and near the top of the 15th century tower is an opening (filled with glass) with a projecting ledge. This was the entrance to an interesting medieval feature — a dove cote — with rows of specially-constructed nest-holes around the bells.

To the south of Collingbourne Wood lies the little town of Ludgershall, once an important settlement during Norman times. During this period a castle was built and for several centuries it dominated the surrounding landscape, playing a major role in the civil wars of Stephen and Matilda and as a royal castle and hunting lodge. It has been a ruin since the 16th century and is the only remaining castle ruin in Wiltshire, other than Wardour Castle. The site having been excavated is now in the hands of English Heritage and visitors can see the large earthworks of the motte-and-bailey castle and the flint walling of the later hunting palace.

Also preserved and standing within railings made by the village blacksmith is the broken shaft of a medieval cross. It has four weatherworn sculptured panels showing the Command of St. Peter, the three Marys, the Ascension, and the Descent from the Cross.

Top right: Shears Inn at Cadley

Walk 11

Distance: *Up to three hours for this five mile walk.*
From the car park of the Shears turn left along the 'dead-end' metalled lane and pass a few brick cottages. The tarmac surface soon peters out, becoming an earth track and bears left with a green sign indicating that your route is a 'road used as a public path'. Almost immediately the track forks; proceed straight on and pass through a metal gate, where a bridleway arrow waymarks you along a delightful green way, along the base of a dry grassy combe. Lush meadows, filled with wild flowers, flank each side of your path and there is the possibility of skylarks serenading you from lofty heights of Sunton Heath to your right.

On approaching a copse, bear off right onto a grassy track, passing between a paddock fence, enclosing an area of wild scrub, and the edge of the copse, which in early summer is abundant with wild rose and elderflower. Your path passes a series of old brush horse jumps, then beyond a gate it bears gradually left with the perimeter of the copse towards another metal gate, situated to the left of a stable/shelter.

a range of sandwiches. The separate restaurant, housed in the old part of the inn, serves more substantial fare such as, steaks, Hungarian chicken paprika, Parson Woodfordes olde English rabbit and onion dish and a selection of puddings from the sweet trolley. Fresh local produce is always used and game is a seasonal speciality. Food is served from 1200-1500 and 1830-2200, although these times are flexible. Walkers can begin their day with breakfast here, for the inn opens at 0900 and stays open throughout the day for coffee, lunch, afternoon tea and supper, closing at 2300. The bar opens at 1100. Children are welcome in the lower restaurant if they are eating and well behaved dogs can come into the bar. Walkers welcome to park in the car park.

Once through the gate, turn right onto a established gravel track that head
steadily uphill, with the line of telegraph poles, into the northern fringes o
Collingbourne Wood. To your left lies an area of neatly planted rows of beecl
trees, aptly named Prancely Rows. The gradient steepens and soon you will cres
the rise and arrive at a T-junction of bridleways. The wide thoroughfare to you
left disappears into the heart of Collingbourne Wood — a vast stretch of Forestr
Commission land and one of the few remaining large areas of woodland that onc
formed the huge hunting forest many centuries ago.

Your route follows the gravel track left, along the edge of Shawdown Copse
Leave the fringe of the wood, then in a hundred yards or so, bear off right at
grassy triangle onto a defined grass centred track and in a little way keep right o
merging with a further by-way. You may feel that you are doubling back o
yourself, but in fact this scenic path is leading you into unspoilt rolling countrysid
that borders the eastern side of Collingbourne Wood. Splendid views soutl
towards Coldridge Wood and the Chutes can be appreciated as you make you
way to a metal gate, where blue bridleway arrows direct you ahead through
peaceful pastoral landscape. No building mars this remote spot, just arable field
heavily dotted with thick copse — Gammon's and Chantry Copse.

Follow the trackway to a further metal gate and pass through a small, predomi
nantly oak, copse on Shaw Down to another gate. It is worth pausing for a fev
moments here, for the rural vista south is even better from the open lofty perch
Your path gently descends through grassland into Shaw Bottom. Go through
gate, then where the main track bears left uphill, just past an old animal pen, keep
ahead to a metal gate and waymarker. Ignore the arrowed path left up the mair
track and the route signed right along the edge of a copse and proceed aheac
through the base of the combe, keeping to the right of the line of wooden posts
What looks like a defined animal track leads you to a metal five-bar gate that flank
the fringe of Hopgood's Copse.

For the first time on the walk your route follows a narrow earth path, which i
summer months can be edged and often obstructed by high nettles, grasses and
abundant cow parsley. Birdsong — chiff-chaffs, willow warblers, wrens and
finches to name a few — should be the only interruption to the peace and quiet o
this isolated valley, as your path widens and enters the fringe of the woodland. The
steep, grassy valley side to your left remains visible for some time, then your patl
begins its passage through Fairoak Copse, an area of woodland that links Coldridg
Wood with Collingbourne Wood. A thick leaf canopy allows water to linger along
the path, so expect a wet and muddy route after prolonged periods of rain. On ou
late spring ramble through this tranquil wooded stretch, we were delighted to see
wild orchids growing in numbers along the edge of the path and evidence of the
fact that areas of the wood are carpeted with a mass of bluebells in early spring

Disregard all the paths and tracks that join your path and eventually emerge ou
onto the gravelled main forest thoroughfare. Turn right, pass to the left of a pole
barrier and follow this wide track through the heart of the wood. The stony

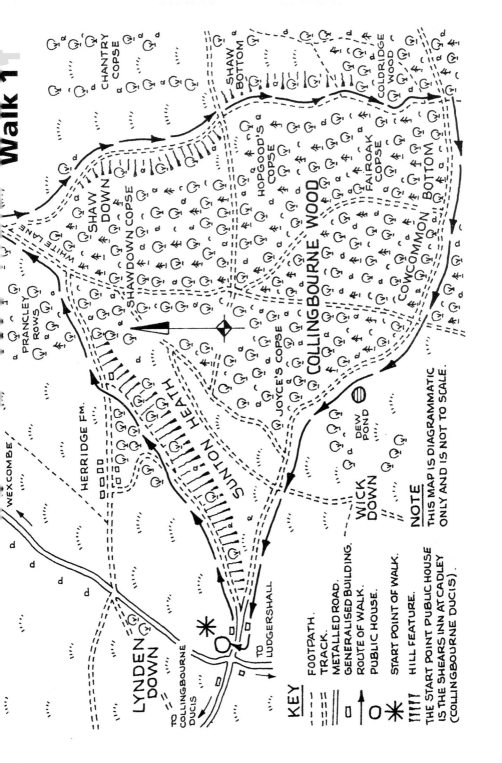

Walk 11

CHANTRY COPSE

SHAW BOTTOM

COLDRIDGE WOOD

SHAW DOWN

SHAW DOWN COPSE

WHITE LANE

PRANCLEY ROWS

WEXCOMBE

HERRIDGE FM.

HOPGOOD'S COPSE

FAIROAK COPSE

COLLINGBOURNE WOOD

COWCOMMON BOTTOM

SUNTON HEATH

JOYCE'S COPSE

DEW POND

WICK DOWN

NOTE
THIS MAP IS DIAGRAMMATIC ONLY AND IS NOT TO SCALE.

LYNDEN DOWN

TO COLLINGBOURNE DUCIS

TO LUDGERSHALL

KEY
- - - FOOTPATH.
= = = TRACK.
≡≡≡ METALLED ROAD.
▢ GENERALISED BUILDING.
↑ ROUTE OF WALK.
O PUBLIC HOUSE.

✳ START POINT OF WALK.

⁗ HILL FEATURE.

THE START POINT PUBLIC HOUSE IS THE SHEARS INN AT CADLEY (COLLINGBOURNE DUCIS).

disturbed soil on th
sunny right-hand edge c
the track supports fox
gloves, wild sweet willian
and to our delight, a mas
of wild strawberry plants
which were rich with
succulent fruit that tastec
heavenly compared to it
cultivated cousin. Th
mixed deciduous tree
fringed track soon be
comes lined with mainl
copper beech as you pro
ceed westwards along
Cowcommon Bottom.

Where the forest tracl
veers sharp left at a cross
roads of paths on the
woodland edge, keep
straight on to follow a de
fined waymarked tracl
between open arable lanc
and Joyce's Copse. Th
passage of farm vehicle
and heavy rain can make
this path awkward to fol
low, especially withou
stout footwear. At the
point where a path forks
off right through the mature, wild rose and honeysuckle-filled hedge, across this
hedge and visible to your left in the field is a dew pond, an unusual feature
sometimes found on chalk downland. The shepherds of old knew the locations o
all these dew ponds, as on the dry heights of the downs they were convenien
watering holes for their stock. Indeed many of the dew ponds were not natura
formations at all but were man-made by local farmers and passing herdsmen.

Maintain your course along this well-established route, eventually cresting the
top of the down, affording open rural views towards Salisbury Plain. With Suntor
Heath to your right, descend the rough track into the valley bottom to a junctior
of routes and your outward path. Keep left and retrace your steps back to the
Shears Inn and your transport.

Bourne Valley footpaths from Hurstbourne Tarrant

WALK 12
Up to 3 hours
5 ½ miles
Walk begins page 73

Background to the Walk

The pretty village of Hurstbourne Tarrant nestles at the bottom of Hurstbourne Hill in one of Hampshire's most unspoilt river valleys, the Bourne Valley. It is the first village of any size that the intermittent and idly flowing River Swift reaches, having risen near Vernham Dean at the base of the remote and wooded chalk hills of North Hampshire. The clear and pure water of the Swift is swelled during the winter months by the delightfully named Bourne Rivulet, which rises near Lower Farm in the village to begin its journey south through meadowland to join the River Test beyond Hurstbourne Priors.

The village, which embraces the idyllic hamlet of Ibthorpe, originated as a Saxon settlement known as 'Hisseburnas' and for centuries its people have been associated with the land, in particular malting, forestry and farming. Vast areas of woodland once supported 22 hurdle makers. The addition of 'Tarrant' to the village name is attributed to the former owner of the manor, for in 1226 the area was granted to a community of Cistercian nuns at Tarrant Crawford in Dorset. Its sister village further down the valley was once owned by the Old Minster in Winchester, hence its name Hurstbourne Priors.

A regular visitor to the village in the early 19th century was the radical reformer and political journalist William Cobbett. He preferred to call the villages Uphusband (Hurstbourne Tarrant) and Downhusband (Hurstbourne Priors), the 'Husband' part of the name being a dialect form of Hurstbourne. Cobbett stayed with his friend Joseph Blount of Rookery Farm (now

Maps
Landranger 1:50,000
Sheet 185
Pathfinder 1:25,000
Sheet SU 25/35
Map Reference of Start/
Finish SU382531

How to get there
Hurstbourne Tarrant is located 5 miles north of Andover on A343 Newbury road. From Andover town centre head north to join A343 for Newbury, then after 5 miles descend Hurstbourne Hill into the village. From Salisbury follow signs M3, A30 London and Andover out of the centre and head north eastwards soon to merge with A343 for Andover. Approaching Andover A343 merges with A303, head west (Exeter) leaving at the next junction and cross A303 to a roundabout. Take the second exit to join the Andover Ring Road and follow A343 Newbury signs around four roundabouts before heading north away from the town to Hurstbourne Tarrant. Hampshire Bus services 30/ 31/31A between Andover and Newbury stop in Hurstbourne Tarrant. Wilts. & Dorset/ Hants. Bus services 7/8/9 and Hants. Bus services 76/76A link Salisbury to Andover as do the trains.

Pub facilities
George & Dragon (Right)
Although this fine 17th Century coaching inn has been refurbished inside, it retains original features which identify it as an historic posting house. Above the inglenook is the mail rack where letters delivered by coach awaited collection. In the Gantry Bar there is an original knee-hole desk where correspondents could pen their missives, and an ancient sash window where mail was accepted. The four comfortably furnished rooms are open to walkers from 1100-1430 and 1730-2300 and in addition to three real ales — Wadworth 6X, Bass and Courage Best — a good selection of home-cooked food is available for hearty appetites. Bar snacks include an excellent range of sandwiches such as chicken, bacon and mayonnaise, roast beef and mustard, while more substantial fare ranges from liver pate and tasty garlic mushrooms for starters, followed by baked chicken breast with garlic and tarragon, steak & kidney & mushroom pie, breast of wood pigeon braised in beer and red wine. Favourites like ham & chips, pasta and burgers feature alongside daily specials such as fish & chips, chilli and broccoli & cauliflower au gratin. Puddings include bread & butter, sticky toffee and Dutch apple pie. Food service 1200-1400 and Wednesday to Saturday evenings from 1900-2115. Children and dogs welcome. Walking eaters and drinkers may use the car park, beneath what is said to be the oldest horse chestnut tree in England.

Rookery House) — a solidly built Georgian farmhouse on the main road at the foot of Hurstbourne Hill — and the village soon became one of his favourites, as is clearly evident in his classic book 'Rural Rides' (1822), which was written at Blount's home. There are no less than 29 references to 'Uphusband' in the book and most are highly appreciative: 'The houses of the village, are in the great part scattered about, and are among very fine and lofty trees; and from many points round about, from the hilly fields, now covered in young wheat, or scarcely less beautiful sainfoin, the village is a sight worth going many miles to see.'

Through Cobbett's book we also learn much about the living conditions in a rural community during the early 19th century for he writes: ' in no part of England have I seen the labouring people so badly off as they are here.' Families were large and conditions in the labourers cottages were primitive.

The church of St. Peter stands in the village street opposite the Bourne Rivulet and was built at the end of the 12th century. It has an attractive weather-boarded bell-turret, erected in 1897 and a predominantly medieval interior. Perhaps the most interesting features in the church are its murals, rare 14th century wall paintings on the north wall, one of which depicts the French legend of 'the three living and the three dead' — three kings out hunting in the forest meet three skeletons which alerts them to their own mortality. Another mural shows the seven deadly sins.

If you explore the churchyard you will find the tomb of William Cobbett's host, ɔseph Blount, who died in 1863. Tradition says he ordered a tombstone big and at enough for the village children to play marbles on.

The George and Dragon, our starting point, dates from the 16th century and is ɪe sole survivor of five inns that once competed for the coaching trade in the illage. Teams of horses were frequently changed here so that fresh animals could ʌckle the severe gradient of Hurstbourne Hill. Joseph Blount often lent his cart-orse to assist the waggoners and, having reached the summit, the horse would e loosed to find his own way home. Inside the inn is the original mail-rack where ɔtters delivered by coach awaited collection.

Our walk passes through the adjoining peaceful hamlet of Ibthorpe, which lies short distance up the valley and consists of a collection of thatched timber-ʌamed cottages dotted around a few fine Georgian farmhouses. Of particular note ɔ Ibthorpe House, once the home of Mary Lloyd, a close friend of Jane Austen — frequent guest of the Lloyd family and later related to them by marriage when ɪ 1797 their daughter wed one of Jane's brothers.

The two settlements are linked by the delightful long-distance walk — the Test Vay — which explores the beauty of the Hampshire countryside from Totton at ɪe seaward end to Inkpen Beacon on the Berkshire border.

Valk 12

Distance: *allow up to three hours for this five-and-a-half mile walk.*

On leaving the George and Dragon turn right and look out for a convenient spot ɔ cross the busy A343 Newbury to Andover road. Once safely on the other side, urn left along the village lane signposted to Ibthorpe, passing the antique shop alled Period Pieces and, a little further on, the village butcher. Before you reach he small bridge over the River Swift, bear off right by the church hall and pass hrough the metal kissing gate to the right of the hall into meadowland.

Your route now bears left along the wire fence behind the hall, then beside the rystal clear water of the Swift. In summer months the river bed could well be dry, ɔut if you are walking this way during winter or early spring, as we were, when he surrounding chalk hills are saturated and the water table is high, both the river hannel and the neighbouring meadows are brimming with water.

Climb a stile and maintain your course parallel with the stream through lush neadowland, with peaceful village scenes away to your left and make for the louble stile ahead. The Test Way logo and green arrow points your way right-ɪanded along the edge of the brook, passing a group of trees called 'John's Copse 969', towards the hamlet of Ibthorpe, nestling in the valley. In the corner of the neadow cross a stile and follow the green arrow left along a farm track, close to ɪ magnificent thatched barn. The track bears right to join the metalled village lane, vhere you turn right to explore the elegant collection of pretty thatched cottages nterspersed with large Georgian houses and some modern dwellings.

Keep to the lane through the hamlet, bearing left where the Test Way is arrowed right up an old unmetalled drove road, to follow it down to the small triangle of grass and the junction with the Upton road. To your right is Ibthorpe House where Jane Austen stayed when visiting the Lloyd family. Your route continues right along the Upton road, across the River Swift, then proceed up valley passing the farm lane for Windmills Farm on your left. In a little way, where the lane begins to bear left, turn left to join a wide hedged trackway, known as Locke's Drove. This ancient routeway gently climbs out of the valley with the wooded slopes of Windmill Hill Down dominating the rural scene away to your left.

Eventually, this tree-lined drove-way follows the dense coniferous woodland fringe to a fork in the track. Here you keep to the left-hand route, maintaining your uphill course along the perimeter of the wood. On reaching a metal barn — Locke's Barn — and a further split in the track, a fingerpost arrows the permissive route right along the woodland edge. Pause a while here to peek through the trees at unspoilt views of the upper Bourne Valley that have unfolded on your right.

The established trackway soon levels out and leaves the wood behind, becoming hedged as it heads towards a green metal shed and a communication mast. Pass Locke's Drove Radio Site and a bungalow, then at a gate beyond linger for a few moments to absorb the superb views north across the rolling downs of the North Hampshire 'Highlands', a mosaic of woodland, ploughland and pasture. The track soon becomes metalled and joins a lane. Turn left, follow the quiet lane and shortly pass Pill Heath Underground Reservoir, a sure sign that you are at the highest point, and a fact that is confirmed by the magnificent vista westwards across Tangley, The Chutes and beyond. The lane then goes over a crossroads, passes Pill Heath House, then in a short distance a footpath fingerpost points you left onto a defined path that runs parallel to a tree-lined hedgerow.

When you reach an area of woodland — Blagdon Copse — keep right-handed along the tree-hedge to a stile in the wire fence on the woodland fringe. Climb the stile and proceed straight on along the left-hand edge of an open arable field, beside the wire fence. To your left, beyond the fence, you may be lucky to see deer feeding on the perimeter of Blagdon Copse, while away to your right there are good views south across Andover and the surrounding countryside.

Soon you will cross a stile flanking a metal gate, then proceed ahead along a defined grass-centred track, bearing right at a junction of routes to maintain your peaceful course along the edge of coniferous woodland. Gently descend to the isolated and deserted Doles Farm. Pass a good barn, then the boarded up brick and flint cottage and keep left at the fingerpost on merging with a farm track. Just beyond a group of holly trees, at a three fingered footpath sign, turn left and follow the path to a stile beside a pair of metal gates.

From here the map clearly shows your path bearing diagonally right across the vast arable field that confronts you. When we walked this way part of the field was very heavily ploughed, with no indication of a path. If this is the case, follow the track along the left-hand hedge, gradually uphill and turn right along a defined farm track that splits the field in two. The track undulates for a short distance, then

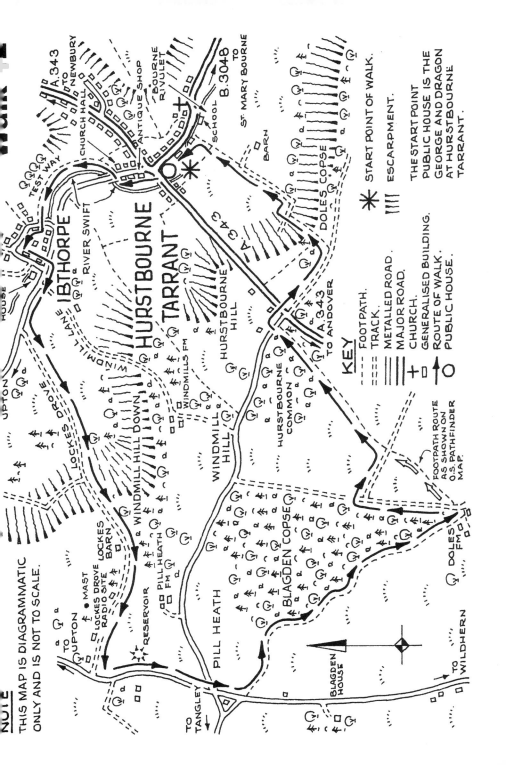

NOTE

THIS MAP IS DIAGRAMMATIC ONLY AND IS NOT TO SCALE.

A.343 TO NEWBURY

ANTIQUE SHOP

BOURNE RIVULET

B.3048 TO ST MARY BOURNE

CHURCH HALL

TEST WAY

SCHOOL

BARN

DOLES COPSE

IBTHORPE

RIVER SWIFT

HURSTBOURNE TARRANT

HOUSE

UPTON

WINDMILL LANE

LOCKES DROVE

WINDMILL HILL DOWN

WINDMILLS FM

HURSTBOURNE HILL

A.343

A.343 TO ANDOVER

HURSTBOURNE COMMON

TO UPTON

MAST

LOCKES DROVE LOCKES BARN RADIO SITE

RESERVOIR

PILL HEATH FM

WINDMILL HILL

BLAGDEN COPSE

DOLES FM

PILL HEATH

TO TANGLEY

BLAGDEN HOUSE

TO WILDHERN

KEY

---- FOOTPATH.
==== TRACK.
|||| METALLED ROAD.
MAJOR ROAD.
+ CHURCH.
□ GENERALISED BUILDING.
↑ ROUTE OF WALK.
O PUBLIC HOUSE.

※ START POINT OF WALK.

))) ESCARPMENT.

THE START POINT PUBLIC HOUSE IS THE GEORGE AND DRAGON AT HURSTBOURNE TARRANT.

FOOTPATH ROUTE AS SHOWN ON O.S. PATHFINDER MAP.

Left: Hurstbourne Tarrant

look towards the wood
land away to your left t
locate a stile on the fiel
edge. On our earl
spring walk, define
tractor tracks clearl
marked the path from
the farm track to the stil
and the edge o
Hurstbourne Commor

Once over the stile a well worn path leads you through the scrub and haze
coppice to a lane, where you turn right to walk the short distance to the A343 an
the top of Hurstbourne Hill. Carefully cross this busy and fast main road onto
clearly waymarked path, the yellow arrow directing you to the left of a gate an
along an established path on the edge of Bourne Park Forestry. It is also known a
Doles Wood, one of the few remaining tracts of woodland that once covered mos
of this region. The area was owned by the crown and used by the various kings fo
their hunting pursuits and the forest also provided work for the villagers, bein
the source of timber for wagon-making and hurdle-making.

Your path soon passes through an old gateway leading you into the woodlanc
fringe and past a small shed. Bear left on merging with a wide forest track, then i
a little way lookout for an ill-defined trackway (not waymarked) branching off t
your left into the trees. A tree to your right has two yellow arrows painted on it anc
marks the point where this track joins the main forest thoroughfare. Gentl
descend to a stile, where a yellow arrow directs you along the now visible path
through the wood towards a wire fence and the woodland perimeter. At the fenc
Hurstbourne Tarrant comes into view, tucked in the valley bottom surrounded b
rolling hills — a most picturesque rural scene.

Yellow arrows keep you on track, directing you steeply downhill along the wir
fence on the fringe of the wood to the base of the hill and an established track. Tur
right, following it left around the field edge, downhill towards the village. Wher
the track bears right to some farm buildings, keep straight on along the fence to
stile, then go across the football field to a stile, which precedes a small paddock
Proceed ahead to another stile, then join a driveway between properties, one a fin
thatched and timbered cottage, and cross the Bourne Rivulet to the village street
If you wish to visit St. Peter's church turn right, otherwise bear left along the lan
and pass Parsonage Farm with its magnificent huge thatched barn and fine timber
framed granary set on staddle stones. Remain on the lane back to the A343 and th
George and Dragon.

A chalk downland walk from Inkpen

WALK 13
At least 3 hours
5 ½ miles
Walk begins page 79

Background to the Walk

Inkpen is not so much a village as an irregular grid of narrow lanes linking clusters of dwellings — Lower Green, Upper Green and Inkpen Common — and old isolated farmsteads that lie at the extreme south-west corner of Berkshire and close to the borders of Hampshire and Wiltshire. The name Inkpen is derived from two Saxon words, 'Inga', the name of a chief and 'pen' meaning an enclosure or stockade — Inga's stockade. Where exactly this stockade was situated is unknown, but the curious terraces on the west side of the old rectory might lead one to suppose that it may have been on that site.

The old rectory, standing on the hill above the church, was built by Colwall Brickenden in 1695, and is a house of great charm. It has a unique garden, designed by the great French designer, Le Notre, who designed and laid out so many gardens for Louis XIV, including the gardens at Versailles.

Beyond the fine tiled-roofed lych-gate with coffin resting board stands St. Michael's church, reflecting architectural techniques and individual taste from the 13th to the 19th centuries. It is a small plain flint and stone building, with the characteristic high-pitched roof of the 13th century and a quaint red-tiled tower. Of particular interest in the church, which was much restored in 1896, is the Early English doorway with a small consecration cross on its left jamb and the great rood screen, carved out of two oak trees, grown on the rectory property. At the west end of the church is the 13th century font, displaying a fine oak cover topped with a sculpture carved in walnut. The carving is called

Maps
Landranger 1:50,000
Sheet 174
Pathfinder 1:25,000
Sheet SU 26/36
Map Reference of Start/
Finish SU359642

How to get there
Inkpen is situated in the
Kennet Valley in Berkshire, 14
miles north of Andover. From
Andover town centre head
north to join A343 Newbury
road and follow it for 5 miles
into Hurstbourne Tarrant.
Turn left onto an unclassified
road signed Upton and
Vernham Dean, then on
reaching Upton turn right for
Linkenholt and Combe to
follow a narrow scenic lane for
another 5 miles to the top of
Inkpen Beacon. Descend the
hill, then at a crossroads, go
straight on into Lower Green.
At the green, bear left for The
Swan. From Salisbury follow
signs north eastwards for M3,
A30 London and Andover,
soon to merge with A343
towards Andover. On joining
A303, head west, exiting at
the next junction to cross
A303, then follow Ring Road
and A343 Newbury signs
around Andover to pick up the
Newbury road and the above
directions.

Pub facilities
Swan, Inkpen (Right)
Set above the village lane, this neat white-painted 17th century farmhouse is the place to come to experience some unusual pub food. The landlord has spent 14 years in the Far East and the cooking in the very comfortable and attractively furnished bars has a strong oriental bias. Exposed beams, four open fires, cushioned pews and benches and an assortment of rustic tables topped with fresh flowers help create a convivial atmosphere in which to enjoy such Singaporean dishes as beef rendang, nsai goreng, lamb keema, Singapore noodles, Maharajah's chicken curry, Szcechuan chicken, sweet and sour fish, mango chicken and stir-fried vegetables. More convential bar snacks including ploughmans, lemon sole, fish and chips and various steaks are also available. The menu features a good selection of vegetarian dishes. To accompany your meal there is a choice of four regularly changing real ales — Brakspears Bitter, Ringwood Best, Old Thumper and Hook Norton Best — at least 14 wines and an interesting range of foreign bottled beers. The bar opens 1130-1430 and 1830-2300 with the normal Sunday hours and food is served daily from 1200-1400 and 1900-2130. Children, but not dogs, are very welcome inside the pub. Al fresco eating and drinking can be enjoyed on the front patio. You are welcome to park your car in the car park, if prior permission is sought.

'In praise of water' and features a series of water-creatures, including a vole, a dipper, a newt, a kingfisher and a teal.

To the west of the church is an ancient drove-way — Bungum Lane — marking the beginning of a linear earthwork, known as The Wansdyke, a huge ditch and bank that stretches to the River Severn via Savernake Forest and the Marlborough Downs. It was constructed sometime after the Romans left the country as some kind of defence or boundary against the early Saxon invasions. At its end, just below the Down, there stood the first house of the Knights Hospitallers, and occasionally, in ploughing the adjacent fields, traces of the foundations are unearthed.

Our walk follows the old drove and climbs to the top of Inkpen Beacon, which forms part of the vast chalk ridgeway that runs east to west through Hampshire, Berkshire and Wiltshire and divides the Thames and Hampshire basins. From the top, at 945 ft., a most exquisite panorama of the English countryside greets the eye, northwards across the green and brown fields and copses of the lush Kennet Valley to the Lambourne Downs, where the Great Ridgeway makes its way to the Thames and south into the undulating Hampshire 'Highlands'. At the highest point, on Gallows Down, is an impressive neolithic long barrow, 6ft. high and 200ft. long.

Standing on top of the barrow is the Combe Gibbet, one of the last grisly landmarks left in England. A great

black cross was first raised here in 1676, which according to local legend was erected to hang a Combe man and his mistress after plotting — successfully — the death of his wife. Felons and highwaymen met their death on the gibbet up to the early 19th century. The existing gibbet is a replica of the original one and the local farmer whose care it is in, has his work cut out protecting it from vandals.

A short distance further east along the ridge is the highest chalk hill in England — Walbury Hill (959ft.) — where there are the obvious remains of a hillfort or camp. It has a single rampart and ditch a mile long in circumference and encloses 82 acres of land, making good use of the steep scarp slope for additional defence. The highlight of this walk are the magnificent all round views from the triangulation point, that can span six counties on a clear day.

Walk 13

Distance: *Allow at least three hours for this five-and-a-half mile walk*
When you leave the Swan turn left along the lane to the green and keep to its right until you reach the T-junction. Here you turn right, signed Ham and Combe and ignore the turning to your left, following the lane round to the right, to where a fingerpost and yellow arrow points you left, beside a house, to a stile flanking a wooden gate. Beyond the stile, you initially follow the left-hand field edge before heading across the pasture towards the large house — the Old Rectory — on the hill. Cross a fence stile in the corner of the field and maintain your course, eventually reaching a stile located beside a metal gate that precedes a lane.

The purpose of coming this way is to visit the tiny 13th century flint church of St. Michael, with its delightful interior and scenic rural aspect and to have a glimpse of the fine Old Rectory. To do this, turn left up the lane and bear immediately right to the splendid church lych-gate. Return to the lane and follow it back downhill, passing a thatched barn prior to reaching a T-junction. Your route heads west out of the village for a little way, to where a footpath fingerpost points you south along an earth trackway, just beyond a wooden fence on your left. Shortly, this established route bears right and becomes grassy as it heads towards the steep scarp slope of Inkpen Hill and the massive chalk ridgeway, which towers over the gently undulating Kennet Valley countryside.

On good breezy days, especially when the wind is blowing from the north, the grassy ridge and sky will be full of multi-coloured parachutes of paragliders. Inkpen Hill is one of the few places in the area where this ever popular sport can be enjoyed, for there is good access and a clear grassy slope. Your track cuts across farmland as it gradually climbs towards the ridge and soon merges with the ancient drove-way called Bungum Lane. Keep ahead at the bridleway sign, the old routeway becoming thickly hedged as it leads you to a small wooden gate at the base of the hill. A blue arrow directs you right, steeply uphill on a defined path, then when you reach a wider path, turn left to follow this diagonally up the scarp slope with magnificent rural vistas unfolding across the Kennet Valley.

This is a strength sapping climb, so regular pauses to catch your breath — either to savour the view or watch with amazement the courage of the paragliders as they launch themselves off the hillside — are much needed. The path soon bears right and begins to level out as your probably now leadened legs carry you to the top of the hill. The panorama from this ridge is stunning as it encapsulates views across a patchwork quilt of fields, hedges and forest, west into Wiltshire and the Vale of Pewsey, north across the Kennet Vale to the Lambourne Downs and to the east into the Thames Valley and the Chilterns.

Having recovered from the climb head west along the grassy ridge, then shortly, bear off left onto a worn path beside Wigmoreash Pond — an old dew pond — to a metal gate. Beyond the gate you join the Inkpen Ridgeway/North Hampshire Ridgeway, an ancient ox-drove that follows the ridge and once used to drive sheep and cattle to the markets in south-east England. Turn left along what can be a very muddy and clayey by-way and follow it east, this time with splendid views south into Hampshire and to the hamlet of Combe, St. Swithun's church and Manor Farm, where King Charles II is supposed to have stayed. The sinister sight of Combe Gibbet, planted in a large Neolithic barrow soon confronts you, its great black cross rearing up against the sky and whistling in the wind to remind us of the macabre days of hanging.

The ridgeway soon becomes the route of the Wayfarers Walk, a long-distance path which begins its traverse of Hampshire from the Gibbet. Maintain your easterly route past the Gibbet and shortly cross the metalled lane which links Inkpen to Combe, then bear off right, with the Wayfarers Walk sign, to follow the

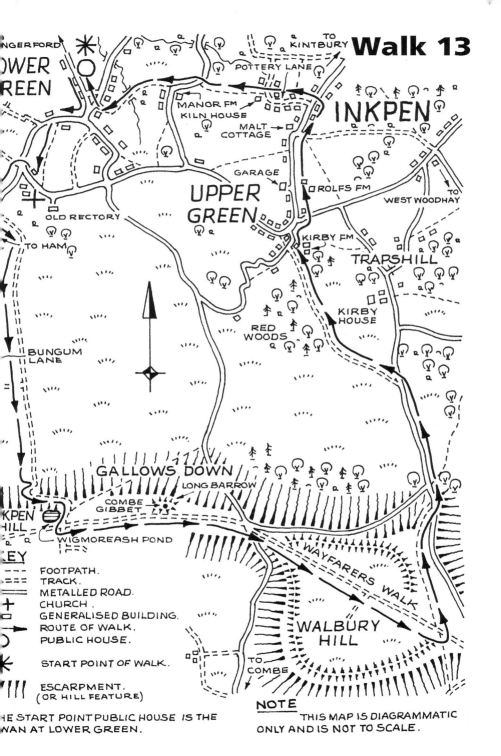

Walk 13

NGERFORD

OWER GREEN

TO KINTBURY

POTTERY LANE

MANOR FM
KILN HOUSE

MALT COTTAGE

INKPEN

GARAGE

ROLFS FM

TO WEST WOODHAY

UPPER GREEN

OLD RECTORY

TO HAM

KIRBY FM

TRAPSHILL

KIRBY HOUSE

RED WOODS

BUNGUM LANE

GALLOWS DOWN

LONG BARROW

COMBE GIBBET

KPEN HILL

WIGMOREASH POND

WAYFARERS WALK

WALBURY HILL

TO COMBE

EY

- - - FOOTPATH.
=== TRACK.
METALLED ROAD.
+ CHURCH.
□ GENERALISED BUILDING.
→ ROUTE OF WALK.
PUBLIC HOUSE.

✳ START POINT OF WALK.

⦚‖‖ ESCARPMENT.
(OR HILL FEATURE)

HE START POINT PUBLIC HOUSE IS THE
WAN AT LOWER GREEN.

NOTE
THIS MAP IS DIAGRAMMATIC
ONLY AND IS NOT TO SCALE.

stony track gently uphill and through the ancient earth rampart of Walbury Camp. This Neolithic hillfort occupies over 82 acres of land and it is worth the short diversion off the main track to locate the triangulation point, which affords unrivalled views.

Leave the hillfort behind and soon lookout for a fingerpost waymarking your route left to a wooden stile, then bear half-left across grassland towards the old ramparts of the hillfort and begin to descend the hillside to a stile. Proceed ahead, your defined path following an old terrace in the hillside, downhill to a further stile, then bear right through the edge of woodland to join a lane. Turn left, then in a little way, keep ahead at the 'give-way' sign, your lane signed to Inkpen. The threatening shape of the hill-top gibbet can still be seen away to your left.

This peaceful lane leads you away from the chalk ridge, then on arriving at a green footpath sign, bear off left onto a grass centred trackway. At a fork in the track, keep right and drop downhill through a copse to a wooden gate, then cross the estate land of Kirby House, the fine Georgian-style house visible to your right. Leave the estate via a pair of wooden gates, then follow the grass centred stony track, which soon passes through a complex of barns to Kirby Farm to a lane. Bear right, then at a T-junction keep right, then shortly turn left along a lane waymarked to Kintbury. Pass the driveway to Rolf's Farm, then a garage specialising in renovating Morris Minors, where a most pleasurable few minutes can be spent viewing the collection of cars on show.

Soon follow the lane round to the right passing the attractive Malt Cottage, then disregard the waymarked path on your right and on reaching the children's playground on your left, turn left with the green fingerpost and blue arrow along a concrete road called Pottery Lane. At the end of this house-fringed lane, pass to the right of a gate to Kiln Cottage and Kiln House and bear right with the gravel drive/track to where a footpath sign arrows you left across a stile in some wooden fencing. Proceed ahead, then follow the left-hand edge of the pasture to what was a broken stile located next to a tree and keep straight on towards a stile beside a metal gate and Manor Farm beyond.

Bear left along a lane, then where it bears left into the farmyard, continue straight on to a stile flanking a gate, then follow the field left-handed to the end of some brick barns and an animal enclosure. Turn left, pass through a gate beside an electricity pylon, then immediately turn right through a further gate, your route waymarked with a yellow arrow onto a wide grassy track between wire fences. When you near a field entrance strung with barbed wire, turn left across a stile and proceed to another stile, then cross a small boggy area before following a defined narrow path through bramble and scrub to a wooden footbridge over a brook. Your worn path then heads right-handed through pasture towards a thatched cottage, then keep to the left of the property along a grassy path between dwellings to join a driveway to a lane. Turn right, then in a short distance turn left at the telephone box and green back to the Swan and your car.

Fields , woods and downland around Pitton

WALK 14
Allow 3 hours
5 ½ miles
Walk begins page 85

Background to the Walk

The parish of Pitton and Farley lies on the boundary of a vast estate — Clarendon Park — which occupies a wide arc of country due east of Salisbury. In Saxon times the area was covered with an ancient forest and within its bounds are the remains of the once magnificent Clarendon Palace, which began its life as a Saxon hunting lodge. It was expanded by the Plantagenets into a great country house, becoming in the 14th century second only to the Palace of Westminster in size and importance.

Many great names in history visited the palace as a place of retreat and pleasure, especially the king and his court who would enjoy hunting in the surrounding forests. The building often suffered long periods of neglect as various kings were absent, either engaged in foreign wars or sorting out domestic disturbances, so it was left to a new monarch to enhance and rebuild the palace. After the War of the Roses, Henry VII had no interest in the palace and it fell into disrepair. So it was in the following century that Queen Elizabeth I, having found it in an uninhabitable state, decided not to rebuild the palace but to abandon it instead.

The archaeologist Dr. Tancred Borenius excavated the site during the 1930s revealing evidence of a Saxon building below Norman foundations. He identified the great hall, the kitchens, the royal quarters and chapel and several council chambers. Almost nothing remains of the palace now, except for only a few feet of flint wall lying only yards from the Clarendon Way, a long-distance walk that traces the old Saxon route which linked Old Sarum to Winchester.

Maps
Landranger 1:50,000
Sheet 184
Pathfinder 1:25,000
Sheets SU 23/33, 22/32
Map Reference of Start/
Finish SU213312

How to get there
Pitton lies 5 miles east of Salisbury. From the city centre follow signs for M3, A30 London and Andover and head north eastwards along A30. Pass under the railway bridge, go over the roundabout beyond following A30 to the top of the hill and take the first turning right, signposted to Pitton. In the village keep ahead uphill for the Silver Plough, which lies on your left. From Andover take A3057 south for Romsey, shortly to join A303 and head westwards. At the next junction take A343 south signposted to Salisbury, passing through Middle Wallop before merging with A30. After a mile, just past the Pheasant Inn, turn left signed Pitton and follow the lane over a crossroads and on for a mile into the village. At the crossroads past the post office turn left uphill for the pub. Bells Coaches service 48 between Salisbury and East Winterslow calls at Pitton and West Winterslow twice daily,

Monday to Saturday.
Hampshire Bus service 32
between Salisbury and
Winchester stops in Pitton.
Andover is linked to Salisbury
by a fast and frequent rail
service, Hampshire Bus
service 76 and Wilts and
Dorset services 7, 8 and 9.

Pub facilities
Silver Plough
This 250-year-old, long white-
painted pub was a farmhouse
up to the Second World War
and in recent years it has
become a quality dining pub,
drawing a discerning clientele
from far and wide for its
award winning food. It has
been Egon Ronay's Pub of the
Year and has merited
inclusion in the Good Food
Guide as well as star ratings
in various other guides. Both
bars and restaurant are neat
and tidy with an assortment of
sturdy tables, chairs, settles
and oak carved benches laid
out beneath a heavily beamed
ceiling, which is festooned
with an array of jugs, mugs,
antique boot warmers,
earthenware and glass rolling
pins. The walls are adorned
with some fine prints and the
snug bar also displays some
cased antique guns and fish.
The restaurant and adjacent
dining area of the lounge has
tables tastefully laid out with
white linen and fresh flowers.
The bar opens from 1100-1500
and 1800-2300 and dispenses
a good range of draught ales,
namely Wadworth 6X, Bass,
Courage Best Bitter and a
guest beer, plus an excellent
selection of wines by the glass
to accompany the imaginative
choice of dishes that are
available on the daily
changing blackboard menus.
(Silver Plough cont.)

The Clarendon Way leaves what is left of the ancien
forest and soon enters the village of Pitton and thi
route, up until the 1920s, was the path that many of the
men of Pitton had to walk in order to earn their 'daily
bread'. Clarendon Woods provided the timber fo
Pitton's important waggon-building and wheelwrigh
businesses as well as for the country crafts of makinε
hurdles, thatching spars, rakes and suchlike.

Pitton and its surrounding area was a favoured spo
for the early settlers as the presence of two buria
mounds on the Winterslow side of the village, the sitε
of a Roman villa near Farley and the discovery of ε
skeleton in the village dating from 1600-1800BC indi·
cate. The first mention of a settlement at Pitton is 841
according to an Anglo-Saxon document and in the 14tt
century it was ministered by the priests of Ivychurcl
Priory at nearby Alderbury. Later the land was ownec
by the Earl of Ilchester, until in 1912 he sold it, givinε
an opportunity for tenant farmers to own their owr
land. Today, Pitton is a substantial village tucked in ε
fold of the South Wiltshire Downs, consisting of a few
old thatched cottages and farmhouses, interspersed
with more modern properties, the result of successfu
infilling in recent years.

The church of St. Peter stands in the High Street ir
the lower part of the village and is older than Salisbury
Cathedral, dating from the 12th century. Built of ε
mixture of greensand, flint and limestone and restored
in 1878, it retains its Norman door and 13th C porch.

Just south of Pitton is the village of Farley, a frag-
mented settlement built around a triangle of lanes witr
a pleasant assortment of buildings. It is known for its
classical church, built of country brick and influenced
by Sir Christopher Wren. It was built for Sir Stepher
Fox who was born in the village of poor parentage, but
being an able and intelligent man he managed to serve
Charles II, eventually rising to Paymaster General. He
later contributed £13,000 to the building of Chelsea
Hospital and in so doing became a friend of Sir
Christopher Wren.

Fox later bought Farley Manor and employed Alex-
ander Fort, an architect who had worked with Wren, tc
build the handsome church between 1689 and 1690

Left: Fox's Fort church at Farley!

Bar snacks are served from 1200-1400 and 1900-2130 and may include chicken noodle soup, lamb and lentil curry, ratatouille Provençal au gratin, Indonesian fish hotpot, avocado, bacon and feta cheese salad as well as ploughmans at lunchtime. The set menu features more elaborate fare such as pan-fried pigeon breast in a port sauce, poached chicken wrapped in olive bread and saute of lambs liver 'Venetian' style, with hot passion fruit souffle and hazelnut praline choux bun for dessert. The restaurant is closed Sunday and Monday evenings. There is a skittle alley and a lawned area at the front. Children are allowed in the snug bar and skittle alley only. Walkers are welcome to park their cars in the car park, if permission is asked first.

The interior has simple panelling and pews, a broad central aisle, some fine monuments and classical-style window glass, giving it the atmosphere and appearance more often found in some London churches. Ten years prior to the building of the church, Fox had commissioned Fort to build the long, low Farley Hospital Almshouses that stand opposite the church. Fox had two sons, one became the Earl of Ilchester — and an owner of Pitton — and the other the First Earl of Holland who had large estates around the parish of Winterslow in the 18th century.

The scattered parish of Winterslow consists of East, West and Middle Winterslow and takes its name from the old English 'wunters hloew' meaning burial ground. Many barrows, flint mines and field systems can be located on the surrounding downs and on Roche Court Down, near East Winterslow, there are Saxon graves.

Our walk incorporates West Winterslow, a hill-top village containing the only Anglican church in the parish, called All Saints, a flint-built structure with a square castellated tower, standing in a clump of beech trees. The exterior of the church was restored in 1866, but the interior retains work from the 13th century and a little Early Norman architecture.

Walk 14

Distance: *Allow three hours for this walk of five-and-a-half miles.*

Taking your leave from the car park of the Silver Plough cross the lane to take the waymarked footpath along the private road, which passes to the left of the village hall opposite. Initially a stony track, it soon becomes grass centred as it passes to the left of a tennis court. Just as you come to the end of the court, bear off left at a small wooden post to join an established footpath that runs through the trees, parallel to the private track. The path eventually passes to the side of a house, then on reaching a fork in the path, bear left through a small copse and negotiate a few fallen trees as you make your way gently uphill to emerge out into pasture.

Your route follows the defined path left-handed along the tree-lined hedge and affords lovely views right to Clarendon Woods, the remnants of a much larger ancient forest. It was once the favoured hunting ground for royalty when they stayed at the magnificent Clarendon Palace, the ruins of which are situated on the far side of the wood. Shortly, in the corner of the field pass through a gap in the narrow hedgerow to join a wide earth trackway at a junction of routes. Keep straight ahead to follow a muddy thoroughfare gradually downhill along the edge of a narrow copse, that was in the process of being cleared and new trees being planted when we passed by.

Stay on this track looking out for a rickety old stile on your left and a yellow arrow waymarking your route half-right, across what was a ploughed field to a stile located to the left of a tree. Climb the broken-stepped stile into a large open arable field and bear half-right to a metal gate and an old stile to its right. The presence of a faded footpath marker instills confidence, confirming that you are still on the right path as you pass through the gate to follow a track along the left-hand edge of a field towards Farley church, now visible ahead. This established track soon becomes hedged and leads you to a quiet lane.

Turn right into the village of Farley, passing the Old Farmhouse and a tumble-down barn before bearing left along Church Road, signposted to Winterslow. Follow the lane around the village recreation field to the handsome brick church and Farley Hospital with its collection of almshouses opposite. Proceed along the lane passing the green corrugated village hall and the school, then just beyond Claremont House turn left along a wide track, waymarked to Pitton and Winterslow. This grass-centred and hedged trackway heads north towards Hound Wood.

When you reach a grassy triangle and a fork in the track on the woodland fringe, keep straight on and enter the coniferous woodland. Stay on the main thorough-fare which bears right through the wood and disregard all the paths to your left and right. Pass numerous log piles, a clearing and some old sheds, your track eventually emerging out of the trees where it becomes grassy as you proceed ahead through pasture. Shortly, the track bears right to follow a hedgerow right-handed along the edge of a large field. Where your defined track bears right beyond an area of newly planted trees, go straight on and maintain your course along the field's edge, this time alongside tree-lined scrub.

As the tree-lined perimeter hedge of the field soon curves left lookout out for a worn path through the hedge boundary and pass into the corner of a further stretch of pasture beyond. Keep left-handed to pick up a clear straight path through the centre of a group of trees, your route being clearly signed at this point. Leave the trees, keep right-handed along the edge of a field, parallel to a line of trees, then where the trees terminate, turn right onto a well established farm trackway that follows the line of telegraph poles uphill through open farmland.

At the top of the rise the track soon veers right away from the route of the poles and later follows a left-hand hedge gently downhill toward West Winterslow.

When you reach the corner of the field, turn left through a metal gate onto what can be, after wet weather, a very muddy and rutted farm access track and head towards a barn. At the barn the track divides, take the left-hand path away from the farm and gradually ascend between lines of trees to a wooden gate. Proceed ahead, ignoring the wide track to your left and waymarked path and stile on your right, to follow a broad thoroughfare that passes to the rear of the houses of West Winterslow. In a little way pass a cabinet makers workshop and the premises of Winterslow Woodcraft, then walk by a bungalow before bearing right downhill towards a lane and All Saints church.

Just past a brick building, before the lane, a footpath sign arrows you left along a grassy path to the rear of the building and the house beyond, then continue straight on keeping to the right of a small silo. Your path follows a hedge left-handed, then heads out across open farmland with good views behind towards the church. You are now following the route of the Clarendon Way.

The defined path soon reaches the far edge of the arable field and follows its right-hand edge for a short way before bearing off right to a stile. Climb the stile, then keep to the worn path along the edge of scrub on top of the steep chalk scarp slope. It is worth pausing here to enjoy the splendid views down into the waterless valley, dotted with farm buildings, and across the rolling downland beyond towards the A30 and Porton Down. At one time a 'winterbourne' flowed from Bentleigh Farm in the valley bottom, through Pitton on its way to Clarendon Lake. This occurred after a succession of wet summers and winters, filling up the 80ft. wells and breaking the surface. It rarely flows nowadays as the water table for some reason has dropped 10ft. or more.

Remain on the path along the top of the slope to a stile, close to a metal gate, and proceed ahead along the fenced path, then shortly turn right onto a wide earth track lined with scrub and yew and head steeply downhill off the chalk down. When you near the base of the hill, at the end of a line of yew, bear off left to join a narrow path that heads towards Pitton, visible in front of you. Shortly, drop down to the right of a bungalow onto a metalled lane. This lane leads you through the top of the village to a T-junction of lanes to the left of the pub car park.

Exploring Grovely Wood from Great Wishford

Background to the Walk

Great Wishford is the most southerly of a delightful series of villages that nestle in the valley of the River Wylye, which gives its name to Wilton and hence to Wiltshire. Knowledge of the village pre-dates the Norman conquest of 1066AD, the written name changing over the years. In the mid 16th century it was Willesford Magna and it was later known as Wishford Magna. Many of the village houses are constructed of Chilmark stone, quarried over the hill in the next valley. Some are interlaced with flint, others are thatched and many are steeply roofed, dating from 1628.

The most interesting cluster of houses is around the church of St. Giles, the original 13th century building being rebuilt in 1863-64, except for the 700-year-old chancel and the 15th century tower. The church houses some interesting treasures, such as the tombs of two old village families, namely the Bonham family, who owned the village from 1278 to the late 16th century and to the successor of the manor, Sir Richard Grobham, who in 1624 is said to have killed the last wild boar in England — or in these parts. It was Grobham who instructed the building of the almshouses that are located to the side of the church. Next door to the almshouses is the village school, made of chequered brickwork and founded in 1722 by Sir Richard Howe for the instruction of the children of the poor.

Also of note in the church is the early Norman font, its sides decorated with ten carved columns, and one of the earliest fire engines made. Made entirely of wood and built by Richard Newsham in 1728, it could provide 65 gallons of water a minute and cost the church-

Maps
Landranger 1:50,000
Sheet 184
Pathfinder 1:25,000
Sheet SU 03/13
Map Reference of Start/
Finish SU078355

How to get there
Great Wishford is situated just off A36 in the Wylye Valley, five miles north west of Salisbury. From the city centre follow signs for The West A30, A303 towards Wilton and Warminster, then on reaching the roundabout, just before Wilton town centre, go straight across to join A36 Warminster road. In 3 miles turn left, signed Great Wishford, enter the village and pass to the right of the church for the Royal Oak, which lies on your right on the edge of the village. From Andover take A3057 south for Stockbridge, then join A303 and head west, before leaving at the first junction to follow A343 towards Salisbury. Merge with A30 and proceed into the city. At the first main roundabout take the fourth exit and follow signs for Warminster and The West. Wilts & Dorset Bus service X4 between Salisbury and Bath, via Warminster calls at Stoford Bridge (A36), from where it is a short walk across

the river into Great Wishford. Hampshire Bus and Wilts & Dorset Bus services 7, 8, 9 and 76/76A link Andover to Salisbury as does a fast rail service.

Pub facilities
Royal Oak, Great Wishford
(Pictured right and far right)
A rambling brick-built pub, it is almost obscured in summer by a very old creeper. Inside, the one main bar features oak beams and wood panelling, wall benches and darkwood furniture and is warmed by an open fire. There is an adjacent lounge and a separate carpeted dining area with huge inglenook and woodburner. An Usher's pub dispensing Courage Best Bitter and Directors, which can be ordered between 1100-1500 and 1800-2300, with the usual Sunday hours. Blackboards display the selection of bar food specials that are available from 1200-1400 and 1900-2200 and may include vegetable lasagne, steak and kidney pie, mushroom and vegetable stroganoff, chilli, tandoori chicken, venison in red wine and chicken breast with prawns and lobster. Lunchtime favourites, such as ploughmans, jacket potatoes and ham, eggs and chips are always on offer. Steaks and grills feature on the a la carte menu. Vegetarians are well catered for — broccoli and mushroom bake, nut and mushroom fettucini — and children have their own menu and are welcome in the bar, as are dogs. A few benches across the lane on a narrow lawn are ideal for fine weather. Walking patrons must ask first to use the large car park at the rear.

wardens £33. 3s. 0d. It may seem hard to believe, but it was used last in 1970 to fight a blaze in the village.

An unusual feature of the village are the stone inscriptions that can be found in the east wall of the churchyard. These tablets record the price of bread in the village since the Napoleonic Wars. In 1801 it was 3s. 10d. per gallon, in 1904 only 10d. and by 1920 it had risen to 2s. 8d.. The 'Gall' measures are a reminder of the days when bread was sold in a semi-liquid form as dough for home baking.

The fact that the village has been in the ownership of just three families over the last seven centuries has meant that many of the ancient rights, customs and traditions have continued to this day. One such old custom takes place on Oak Apple Day — May 29th — when villagers commemorate the victory over the local landowner, the Earl of Pembroke, who in creating Wilton Park closed the east-west road, south of the River Nadder, thus interfering with their ancient rights — from a charter granted in 1603 — to cut and gather wood in nearby Grovely Wood.

Celebrations begin at dawn when the young people of the village wake each household in turn by banging tin pans and shouting 'Grovely, Grovely, Grovely and All Grovely'. Armed with billhooks and accompanied by musicians, they walk up Grovely Lane into the woods, where they cut green branches for their houses and a larger bough for the church tower. Until recently villagers dressed in costume and led by the Rector,

hen went on to Salisbury Cathedral, where further celebrations, in the form of
ancing, occurred before the High Altar and in the Close. Today, festivities are
onfined to the village, where a procession winds its way around the village,
nding up in Oak Apple Field. Here there are competitions, games, dancing
round the Maypole and refreshments. The day's event is recorded in the pub sign
f the Royal Oak.

Another custom of bygone days is the Midsummer Tithes auction just before
unset on the Monday of Rogation Week, in late April or May, when the grazing
ights on two small pastures from Rogationtide to August 12th are sold. The
auction is conducted by the churchwarden, who walks up and down the church path collecting the bids. The moment the sun vanishes below the horizon he knocks down the bargain to the last bidder, using the church key as a gavel.

Left: Stone plaques with bread prices on the east wall of the churchyard.

The Avenue — 'Grovely, Grovely, Grovely and all Grovely'

Walk 15

Distance: *Allow up to three hours for this walk of five-and-a-half miles.*

From the Royal Oak turn right along Grovely Lane, passing under the railway bridge to leave the village confines. Follow this delightfully quiet dead-end lane through farmland, gradually climbing up a sheltered combe — Penning Bottom — towards Grovely Wood. On a fine, warm spring day, skylarks singing high in the sky accompanied us as we strolled along this beautiful route, leaving the Wylye Valley behind.

The tarmac soon peters out to a wide stony trackway as you enter Grovely Wood, a fine stretch of woodland that was once a royal hunting forest, which together with the New Forest and Cranborne Chase, formed a very significant preserve. Initially, the wood is a splendid mix of trees, such as silver birch, larch, hazel, oak, rowan and ash, providing a superb habitat for a variety of birdlife, from woodpeckers and colourful jays, to finches and many summer songbirds and warblers.

Your peaceful ramble, although free from traffic noise, may be interrupted by a passing RAF jet on a practice flight from a nearby airbase. The track soon becomes metalled once more and begins to climb steadily uphill to the top of the ridge. When you reach a fork, continue straight on, the bright colours of rhododendrons fringing your path in spring as it levels out on top of the hill, which divides the Wylye and Nadder Valleys.

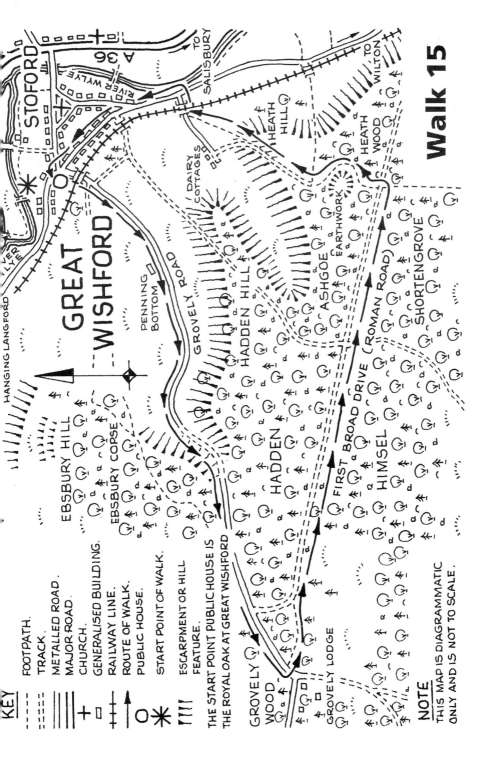

Walk 15

KEY

- - - - - FOOTPATH.
- – - – - TRACK.
≡≡≡ METALLED ROAD.
≣≣≣ MAJOR ROAD.
✝ CHURCH.
☐ GENERALISED BUILDING.
+++ RAILWAY LINE.
→ ROUTE OF WALK.
○ PUBLIC HOUSE.
✳ START POINT OF WALK.
❙❙❙❙ ESCARPMENT OR HILL FEATURE.

THE START POINT PUBLIC HOUSE IS
THE ROYAL OAK AT GREAT WISHFORD

NOTE
THIS MAP IS DIAGRAMMATIC
ONLY AND IS NOT TO SCALE.

STOFORD

A 36

RIVER WYLYE

TO SALISBURY

HANGING LANGFORD

GREAT WISHFORD

EBSBURY HILL

EBSBURY COPSE

PENNING BOTTOM

GROVELY ROAD

DAIRY COTTAGES

HADDEN HILL

HADDEN

ASHGOE EARTHWORK

HEATH HILL

HEATH WOOD

TO WILTON

SHORTENGROVE

FIRST BROAD DRIVE (ROMAN ROAD)

HIMSEL

GROVELY WOOD

GROVELY LODGE

Shortly, look out for a yellow arrow on a telegraph pole to your right, waymarkin you left in a few yards, onto a narrow, worn path through the trees. This delightfu shady way follows a line of mature beech trees and should, if you are not makin too much noise, afford the chance to view some deer feeding in the clearings t your left and right. Your path soon merges with a stony track, bear right toward a metal barrier and a 'private woods' sign. Pass to the right of the barrier to join magnificent straight copper beech-lined avenue through the heart of the woo called First Broad Drive.

This splendid wide avenue is part of the old Roman Road, or Lead Road, whic linked the lead mines of the Mendips in Somerset to Wessex, where it joined othe ancient routes, such as the Harrow Way to Kent. Walking this way on a hot sprin day, this shady broad ride provided a welcome respite from the heat and prove to be a delightful stretch of the walk. Peace and quiet allowed us the opportunit to observe deer in the clearings on the left-hand side, which were resplendent wit tall foxgloves. The mixed woods and tracks on either side of you are private, s keep to the pitted central track, ignoring the first crossroads of public path arrowed in blue and continue along the avenue. When you reach the next po displaying yellow footpath arrows, turn left to follow a leafy well used bridlewa — which can be muddy at first — through the trees. Keep ahead where it fork then at the next split in the path, bear right with the yellow arrow onto a narro path, which according to the Pathfinder map, crosses an old earthwork. Where thi main path bears sharp right, proceed ahead to a stile visible on the woodlan fringe. It is worth pausing for a few moments here, for the view into the Wyly Valley to the villages of Great Wishford and Stoford and across the rollin downland beyond is quite superb.

Climb the stile, turn diagonally left to a fence stile located beside the wire fenc on the woodland edge, then follow the pasture edge left-handed to where the pat reaches a cluster of trees. Here, bear off half-right through grassland towards th first tree along the perimeter fence of the field. Pass through a fence stile to join well established grassy track, which follows the top of Heath Hill, then descend into the bottom of the valley, to a stile located beside an open field entrance Beyond the stile, head straight across lush pasture towards the railway bridge i the far left-hand corner. Go over the stile, bear right under the railway, then at th T-junction of lanes, turn left along a quiet lane, parallel with the River Wylye fo a short distance before entering Great Wishford. Remain on the lane, whic eventually leads you back to the crossroads beside the Royal Oak.

Avon Valley paths from Upper Woodford

WALK 16
Allow 3 hours
6 miles
Walk begins page 97

ackground to the Walk

he course of the River Avon flowing south across the
alisbury Plain, is diverted suddenly by the broad
houlder of Amesbury Down. From here this clear
halk stream meanders through the most idyllic and
nspoilt Woodford Valley for seven miles into the city
f Salisbury. The peacefulness of the this part of the
alley contrasts with the Upper Avon, north of
mesbury, where military establishments and hous-
g have developed rapidly since the 1950s. This is due
a succession of landowners and tenant farmers, who
rcupy a series of small manors and farms throughout
ie valley, resisting change and preserving a unique
enic landscape.

Thankfully, the two main roads to Salisbury follow
ie downland ridges on either side of the valley, leav-
g the Woodford Valley well off the beaten track. A
ries of tiny lanes follow almost every twist and turn
f the river, passing through lush river meadow pas-
ire, interspersed with mature trees and rows of weep-
g willow, marking the river's course. These lanes link
string of straggling picturesque villages, where at-
active thatched cottages, impressive manor houses
id ancient churches nestle beside the shallow fast-
owing River Avon.

At the Woodfords — Upper, Middle and Lower —
ad and river almost touch and the river is wide
hough to require three arches to the bridge. The
mmunities are essentially agricultural in character,
ch having large farms incorporated in the fabric of
e village. Between Middle and Upper Woodford,
cked down by the river's edge and sheltered by trees

Maps
Landranger 1:50,000
Sheet 184
Pathfinder 1:25,000
Sheet 03/13
Map Reference of Start/
Finish SU372124

How to get there
Upper Woodford is five-and-a-
half miles north of Salisbury.
Head north, leaving the Ring
Road to join A345 for
Amesbury and Marlborough.
Pass Old Sarum, then after 2
miles at the High Post Hotel,
turn left for Netton and
Woodfords. At a T-junction in
Netton, turn right and shortly
across the Avon to The Bridge
pub opposite. From Andover
follow signs for A303 Exeter.
Head west on the dual
carriageway until you reach
the first roundabout on the
outskirts of Amesbury. Turn
left onto A345 and head south
through the town and across
Amesbury Down to the High
Post Hotel. Turn right for the
Woodford Valley and Upper
Woodford. Wilts & Dorset
Bus service 1 Salisbury—
Amesbury stops in the villages
in Woodford Valley. Wilts &
Dorset/Hants Bus services 7,
8, 9 between Salisbury and
Andover stop in Amesbury
and 76/76A link Salisbury
and Andover, as does the
railway.

Pub Facilities
Bridge at Woodford,
Upper Woodford

(Pictured right)
A white-painted laneside inn in an enviable location opposite the River Avon. A delightful large lawn with picnic benches and brollies is set right on the riverbank and is a very popular summer drinking spot, seating 150 people. Neatly refurbished main bar with pine tables, old pews and comfortable wall bench seating, a candle-lit dining room, an intimate 'snug' room with a collection of books (some for sale) and an adjoining games room with pool table. The bar opens from 1100-1430 and 1830-2300, with the usual Sunday hours and serves the Gibbs Mew range of ales — Salisbury Best and Wiltshire Bitter. A comprehensive printed menu is available throughout opening hours and features filled rolls and French sticks, salads, a range of steaks, jacket potatoes and chef's specials — lasagne, chicken Kiev, beef and Guinness pie, chilli, chicken curry and at least four vegetarian choices. Daily blackboard specials enhance the menu with dishes like Wiltshire Pie, seafood tagliatelle, fishermans platter, chicken satay and the impressive Bridge Inn ploughmans — home-made quiche, slice of gammon ham, chunk of mature cheddar, local pickles, salad and fresh bread. Children are welcome in the games room, in the snug and in the dining room. Live jazz can be heard on Sunday evenings during July and August. Note: the car park is locked outside opening hours.

is the 17th century Heale House, a fine brick hous enlarged in 1894 by Detmar Blow. Much of the hous (not open) is unchanged since King Charles II sougl refuge here after the Battle of Worcester in 1651. Th eight acres of gardens are open daily — 1000-1700 — a year, and allow the opportunity to view the wonde fully varied collection of plants, shrubs and musk an other roses, growing in the formal setting of clippe hedges and mellow stonework.

The walk explores a few of the manor dominate hamlets, located north of the Woodfords. The first i the community of Lake, its name referring to a forme tributary of the Avon, now only a dry valley, known a Lake Bottom. The most prominent building is Lak House, a well restored 16th century flint and ston mansion, complete with turrets and crenallations an built by a wealthy clothier George Duke.

A little further up the lane is Wilsford Manor, splendid neo-Jacobean mansion, built of chequere flint and stone in 1906. One former resident, Sir Olive Lodge, was one of the pioneers of the wireless ag aiding Marconi in making broadcasting a reality. H died aged 90 and is buried in the tiny church of S Andrew next door, which retained its quaint Norma church tower despite extensive Victorian 'restoratior at the end of last century. The only village we visit o the east side of the river is that of Great Durnforc which lies beneath the Iron Age hillfort of Ogbury Camp. This encompasses over 62 acres, much of it now farmland. Formerly known as Much Durnford and Hungerford Magna, after the family who once held it, Durnford means 'secret' or 'hidden' ford. The ford was possibly by the orchard behind the church, although there is no crossing of the Avon here today. It is a most attractive settlement of old-world thatched cottages, with a fine manor and one of the most notable churches in the valley — St. Andrew's. It boasts some ancient wall paintings, a splendid carved Norman chancel arch and a Norman font with an array of interlaced arches.

Walk 16

Distance: *Allow three hours for this ramble of six miles (Plus 3 mile Stonehenge detour)*
As the pub car park is locked outside opening times please check with the pub before leaving your car there — you may be able to leave it there in the afternoon and collect it when the pub re-opens. On leaving The Bridge, turn left along the lane towards the main village centre passing Boreland Farm, then when you reach Boreland House on your left, turn right onto a grass centred gravel track. A short diversion further along the lane will bring you to an unusual farm outbuilding that boasts a neo-Georgian clock tower, which was erected in 1935 to commemorate George V's Silver Jubilee. Back on the track, follow it round to the right, then left to pass a group of old sheds and shortly reach a further track leading to a house on your left. Turn left for a little way, before bearing off right onto a grassy thoroughfare where the track veers sharp left, near a tennis court.

Your route now heads up valley along this delightful path, affording serene and lush river meadow scenes with weeping willow trees marking the course of the Avon. Soon you will pass the fringe of a group of poplar trees and the crystal clear shallow water of the river can be glimpsed, as it threads its way down this unspoilt valley. The path narrows and drops down to the river's edge, disregard the path on your right that leads to a small footbridge over the river and proceed along what can now be a muddy and nettle-lined bridleway that gradually climbs up the valley side, away from the river. Cross a metalled driveway, your narrow path soon becoming edged with trees to your right, allowing cameo rural views across the valley towards Great Durnford, nestling on the eastern bank of the river.

Pass a thatched cottage — Lake Hill Cottages — and cross the lane to a stile flanking a metal gate, then head straight on through pasture, between a line of mature oaks and a wood. A magnificent view north up the Avon Valley, towards Amesbury and beyond across the open and rolling Salisbury Plain, can be appreciated at this point, your foreground scene dominated by the splendid 16th century flint and stone Lake House. Gently drop down to a gate and stile, then descend through woodland, shortly bearing right out into an arable field, your path following its right-hand edge down into Lake Bottom. Go through a small wooden gate and turn left onto an established grass centred trackway that follows the bottom of this peaceful dry valley. It was once a tributary of the Avon, fed by a multitude of springs from the surrounding chalk downs.

Your track soon bears right by a group of trees that shield the crumbling remnants of an old wellhouse — Lake Wellhouse — and becomes a wide grassy green way, that wends its way along Lake Bottom, between downland arable fields. Used frequently by horses this sheltered route soon passes through Spring Bottom, between a paddock and woodland, before bearing left toward Springbottom Farm and a junction of tracks. At this stage of the walk a long deviation from the main route can be taken by turning left, away from the farm to follow the wide track across Normanton Down to Stonehenge (1·5 miles).

If lack of time or energy does not allow such a diversion, turn right to follow the metalled driveway past the barns and farmhouse, then just before you bear right with the drive at the base of a long hill, bear off left to join a narrow earth path that climbs parallel to the driveway through a line of trees. We found this path far less strength sapping and soul destroying compared to the long climb up the metalled road, especially on a hot June day. Your endeavours are rewarded as you near the top of the down, for a break in the tree-line allows the opportunity to pause for a few minutes to appreciate the magnificent panorama north, towards Stonehenge and beyond to Salisbury Plain.

On the downland — Normanton Down — to your left there can be seen numerous clusters of Bronze Age tumuli or burial barrows. Around Stonehenge there are over 310 barrows in twelve square miles, the densest collection in Britain; Normanton Down has a group of thirty. Also at this point, when we walked this way, there was a protest board informing walkers of the proposed new route of the A303, when it is diverted away from Stonehenge. Photographs indicate the route and markers are visible through the fields in front of you.

At the top of the hill, opposite some large farm buildings, your path joins the metalled road, then begin your descent back into the verdant Avon Valley. During weekdays the peace and tranquillity of the valley is often shattered by the passage of noisy jets on practice flights from Boscombe Down, located on the opposite side of the valley. When you reach the valley bottom road at Wilsford, turn right for a short way if you wish to visit St. Michael's church. The church door is generally kept locked, but the key can be obtained from the Red House, located 100 yards on your right after leaving the churchyard. Your main route heads north along the road into the hamlet of Normanton, then on reaching the postbox turn right to follow a waymarked path through large metal gates and along a tree-lined driveway. When you near the property, bear off left to a stile flanking a metal gate then walk beside a thatch-topped wall and garden, shortly to cross a small brick bridge before bearing left towards a metal gate and the River Avon.

It is well worth stopping and relaxing here, for this stretch of river bank is truly delightful, a peaceful and secret place to sit and savour the beauty of the Avon and its wildlife. Our summer sojourn here revealed a family of swans, coots, moorhens, grey wagtails, spotted flycatchers, swallows and swifts, a kestrel and numerous warblers and wrens flitting among the reeds. Pass through the metal gate, cross the bridge over the river, then follow a narrow earth path, that threads

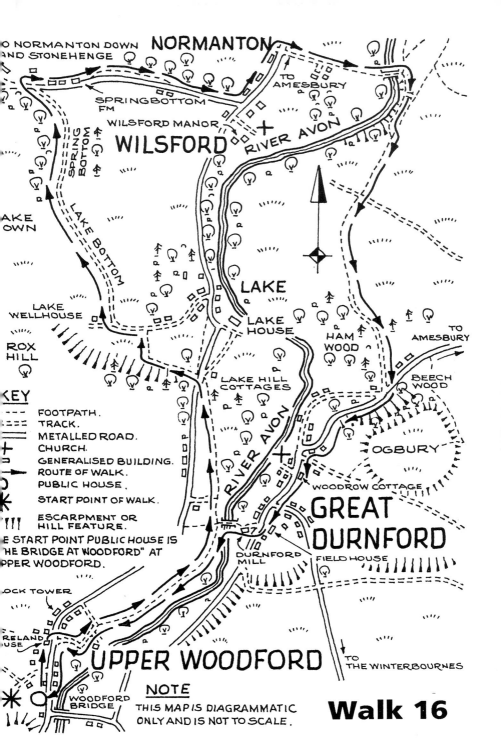

Walk 16

its way through a group of popular trees to a wooden footbridge of a tributary stream. Once over the bridge, bear right along an ill-defined path beside the stream. High nettles may force you to walk higher up along the steep bank, then cross the roots of a fallen tree and emerge out into lush grassland. Keep

near the base of the valley side and trace the narrow grassy path that soon gradually climbs out of the valley, parallel with a wire fence.

When you reach the top a blue bridleway arrow directs you through an old metal gate, then along the left-hand edge of a crop field. With superb Avon Valley views proceed across a grass centred track, then keep left-handed through a further arable field, alongside a hawthorn hedgerow, towards woodland. On nearing the woodland fringe, bear off left through the hedgerow to a metal gate. A blue arrow waymarks you along what can be an overgrown path, which affords views across the valley to Lake House looming above the trees and soon merges with a well-defined track. Keep left and remain on this route through the edge of Ham Wood, eventually heading downhill to a lane.

Across the lane on the hill in Beech Wood, but not visible, is the site of Ogbury Camp, an ancient hill-fort. Turn right along the lane, pass the entrance to Great Durnford Manor and proceed along this undulating lane into the village of Great Durnford. Old-world thatched cottages with colourful, flower-filled gardens abound and also worth viewing is the historic church of St. Andrew, a real gem of a church in this valley and located down the lane on your right opposite Woodrow Cottage. Walk through the village passing the cricket ground and the turning for the Winterbournes, then proceed beyond the Black Horse to where a footpath fingerpost, opposite Field House, arrows you right towards Durnford Mill.

A poplar-lined grass-centred track leads you to the mill, where you bear off right, just before the gravel drive, to follow a fenced path that soon crosses the bridge over the millrace and the main stream. Overhanging willow enhance attractive and serene river scenes and yet again we succumbed to the temptation to linger on the bridges over this jewel of a chalk stream. With evening opening time at The Bridge nigh and the demand for a riverside bench high, we crossed to the west bank of the river and turned left to re-join our outward route and the three-quarter mile stroll back to the pub.

est Valley paths
nd downland tracks
rom Stockbridge

WALK 17
At least 4 hours
7 ¹/₂ miles
Walk begins page 103

ackground to the Walk

his walk explores the beauty of the Test Valley, its mous chalk stream — one of England's great rivers, ·nowned around the world for its trout fishing — and ·turns along ancient tracks that criss-cross the sur-)unding rolling chalk downland.

  Stockbridge is a large village sited upon a great ·tificial chalk causeway that stretches for half-a-mile :ross the soft peat of the valley. To fishermen it is the ndisputed 'capital' of the Test Valley. It was during le 10th century that a frontier stronghold was built on le causeway by the Saxons to defend Wessex from the 1arauding Danes. Later it became a major routeway nking Winchester to Old Sarum.

  The village developed rapidly, becoming a borough s long ago as 1256 and from 1563-1832 it had two 1Ps. From the time of Henry III until the coming of the ailways, Stockbridge was an important resting place)r Welsh drovers, as they journeyed across the breadth f England to the great fairs and markets in Surrey and .ent and sheep markets were held regularly in the ongested main street. On the west side of the village, short distance along the Houghton road, is a thatched ottage that was once an inn used by the Welsh drov- rs. Its facade is inscribed with a few Welsh words, vhich, roughly translated, mean 'seasoned hay, tasty)astures, good beer, comfortable beds'.

  When the droving declined, Stockbridge maintained ts importance and wealth by becoming a famous horse- acing centre in the 19th century. Between 1753 and 898 a racecourse existed high on the Downs at)anebury and a frequent visitor was the Prince of

Maps
Landranger 1:50,000
Sheet 185
Pathfinder 1:25,000
Sheet SU23/33
Map Reference of Start/
Finish SU355352

How to get there
Stockbridge lies in the heart of the Test Valley between Salisbury and Winchester. From Salisbury follow signs M3, A30 London and Andover out of the centre and head north eastwards along A30 for 7 miles, then where A30 merges with A343, turn right signed Stockbridge and Winchester and remain on the A30 for 11 miles into Stockbridge. From Andover head south on the A3057 signed Stockbridge and Romsey and follow it for seven miles through the Test Valley into the village. Hampshire Bus service 32/34 between Salisbury and Winchester stops in Stockbridge and service 99 links Andover to Stockbridge.

Pub facilities
Greyhound, Stockbridge
With 300 yards of private fishing on the Test, this 15th century pub is a popular haunt for fishermen, who make good use of the accommodation and facilities

here. The comfortable carpeted main bar has beams, a brick fireplace with warming winter log fire and a collection of old tables and chairs. It is an Ushers house serving their Best Bitter, Founders Ale, Courage Best and Directors between 1100-1430 and 1545-2300 Monday to Friday and 1100-2300 on Saturdays. Of note on the printed menu are the pies — New Forest game, steak and oyster, chicken and mushroom — a good range of soups, sandwiches and ploughmans. Blackboard specials include chicken curry, lasagne, pork escalope, Dover sole and of course fresh Test trout, available from 1200-1400 and 1900-2100 (2130 Saturday). Children are welcome in the back lounge and dogs are allowed in the bar.

Vine, Stockbridge
Cream-painted inn with attractive bow windows and High Street views. The comfortable, well decorated and beamed interior has a brick fireplace, exposed brick walls and plenty of prints, tankards and other nick-nacks adorning the bar. Good winter log fires. The bar opens from 1100-1430 (1500 Saturday) and 1800-2300, with the usual hours on Sunday and dispenses a good selection of real ales — Boddingtons, Wadworth 6X, Twelve Bore and a regular guest ale. Bar food is very popular, the bar menu may feature French onion soup, croissant filled with smoked chicken and tarragon mayonnaise, hot lamb curry, ham, egg and chips and various ploughmans, salads, jacket potatoes and sandwiches.

Wales (Edward VIII), who stayed at Hermit Lodge – named after the Derby winner of 1867 — on th Houghton road. At its peak the area had no less tha nine racing stables. The demise of horse-racing wa stimulated through better transport facilities to suc major venues as Ascot and the development of a large racecourse at nearby Salisbury.

During this period Stockbridge's other sport flour ished and the River Test has since become the mos exclusive and expensive fishing river in the world. Th oldest and most select fishing club in the world — Th Houghton Club — founded in 1822, has by traditio just 17 members.

The long main street crosses at least six branches c the River Test and is lined with a mixture of cottages small houses and shops, interspersed with a brick tow hall, built in 1810 and dominated by the imposing 17t century Grosvenor Hotel and its huge porch sup ported by columns. The room above the porch is th headquarters of The Houghton Club.

Just south of the village your walk joins the Tes Way, a long-distance walk which traverses Hampshir from north to south. At this point on its route it follow the disused Test Valley Railway, affectionately know as the 'Sprat and Winkle Line', for a distance of 1(miles. The railway, built in 1865, replaced the old cana that ran between Redbridge and Andover and close in 1964. In many areas of Britain, country lovers — especially walkers — have benefited since Beechin axed many of the branch lines, for numerous old route have been opened up for recreational purposes. The route of the old railway affords some of the best view across this tranquil river valley and harbours a diverse selection of flora and fauna.

On the other side of the valley is the straggling village of Houghton, its long main street lined with a assortment of thatched, brick and timber-framed and Edwardian houses. Of note, are the red-brick vicarage and Manor House and All Saints church, which has a 19th century timber spire and shingled tower. If you venture to the northern edge of the village, you wil find Houghton Lodge, an 18th century fishing lodge boasting some fine riverside and walled gardens.

Restaurant fare ranges from halibut steak with an Indian sauce and lamb cutlets with garlic and rosemary sauce to steak topped with cambozola, with apple pie and chocolate pot to finish. Food is served 1200-1415 (1430 Saturday and Sunday) and 1830-2130 (1900-2200 Friday and Saturday). Children have their own menu. Dogs are not welcome inside.

Boot Inn, Houghton
(Pictured above left) The pub used to be the HQ of the Houghton Fishing Club before it moved to Stockbridge. Today, the neat open-plan interior is a popular dining venue and the riverside garden a favourite spot for a summer drink. There are two distinct food operations here; the bar menu is available throughout the pub at lunchtimes — ploughmans, omelettes, lasagne, Cumberland sausages — with a separate restaurant menu introduced in the evenings. Fresh fish is featured well — red mullet, Dover sole, moules — and interesting meat dishes such as rack of lamb in a port wine sauce and breast of duck with blueberry sauce. Specials boards change daily and may include game pie, steak and kidney pie, local sausages, a fresh fish choice and puddings like Hawaiian apple pie. Bar opens 1100-1500 and 1830-2300 with food being served from 1200-1430 and 1900-2200. On draught are Boddingtons Bitter, Wadworth 6X, Eldridge Pope Royal Oak. Well behaved children and dogs are welcome inside. Walkers are welcome to park in the car park, if prior permission is sought.

High up on the downland, north-westwards of Stockbridge is the ancient earthwork of Danebury. This hillfort is a magnificent sight, with a double bank and ditch and an inner rampart up to five metres high, which is covered with beech trees. It was occupied by the Atrebates, a Celtic people, from about 550BC to 100BC and excavations have revealed a detailed picture of Iron Age society. Discoveries include a pattern of streets, circular houses, shrines and storage pits and over 100,000 pieces of pottery. It is owned by Hampshire County Council and the site is open to the public. Many of the best finds are exhibited in the Iron Age Museum in Andover.

Walk 17

Distance: *Allow at least four hours for this seven-and-a-half mile ramble.*

Feeling suitably refreshed and having perused the buildings and shops along the main street, make your way to the old Waggon and Horses pub — now Lillie Bakery and Tearooms — located mid-way along the south side of the street. A black-painted fingerpost on the pavement waymarks your path alongside the bakery to a metal swing gate, then onto a tarmac path beside one of the crystal clear streams of the River Test that flow beneath the village. Shortly, you will cross a footbridge and stile to join a well worn path across pasture, leaving the village behind.

Beyond a further kissing gate and concrete footbridge over Marshcourt River -
a sizeable gently flowing channel of water that feeds the Test — a board notifie
you that you are entering Common Marsh, an area of beautiful riverside meado
rich in wild flowers, that is in the safe hands of the National Trust. It is one of tl
few places along the length of the Test, especially in this area, that one can actual
walk beside the trout-filled waters for the banks are generally private, reserve
exclusively for wealthy fishing syndicates. The reason for its accessibility date
back some 900 years when the land was granted to the lords of the manor b
charter, allowing citizens of Stockbridge to use it to graze their cattle — up to s
beasts each. In March the manorial court meets to decide on the number of anima
to be allowed on the pasture.

The delightful springy turf path follows the reed-fringed clear waters of tl
river channel, which is haven to a variety of birds such as coots, moorhens an
wagtails and affords some splendid valley views back towards Stockbridge. Sadl
the joys of the riverbank are short-lived, at least for the walker, as the tranqu
water's edge path becomes the preserve of the fishermen. Bear left with the wid
grassy swath, following the fence towards a stile.

Looming above the trees in front of you are the towering chimneys of Mars
Court, a grand white house which was designed at the turn-of-the-century fc
Herbert Johnson by the famous architect Sir Edwin Lutyens. The house is unusua
for it is built entirely of chalk and the gardens, designed by Gertrude Jekyll, consis
of a maze of terraces, sunken gardens and decorative brick paths. Since the last wa
it has been used as a hospital, refugee centre and more recently as a school. At th
time of our walking this way it was up for sale.

Once you are over the stile, turn right along the Test Way to follow the old cours
of the Test Valley Railway. This peaceful level route follows the valley edg
southwards through some of Hampshire's finest unspoilt countryside. Walkin
the old railway stimulates the imagination, recreating the atmosphere and scene
of the days of steam when passengers enjoyed the same cameo views across th
serene river meadow landscape from a slow moving train. Today, the scrut
thickets and grassy banks bordering the old line and watermeadows harbour
wealth of fora and fauna. Primroses line the old banks in early spring an
nightingales can be heard in May, when they are in full song as dusk begins to fal

Remain on the Test Way until you reach a four-fingered fingerpost and
crossroads of tracks. Turn right following the track waymarked 'Clarendon Way'
the long-distance path that links Salisbury with Winchester. The well established
track takes you across the broad expanse of watermeadow and over three bridge
which span the river channels of the Test. It is worth lingering awhile on thes
bridges for the river scenes are truly peaceful. Reeds and willow border the clea
waters of the Test and trout can often be seen swimming in the shallows.

After crossing a wooden footbridge, follow the track to a metal gate, pas
through the gap to its left and turn right along the lane, you are now in the villag
of Houghton. Keep to the footway through the long, straggling village until you

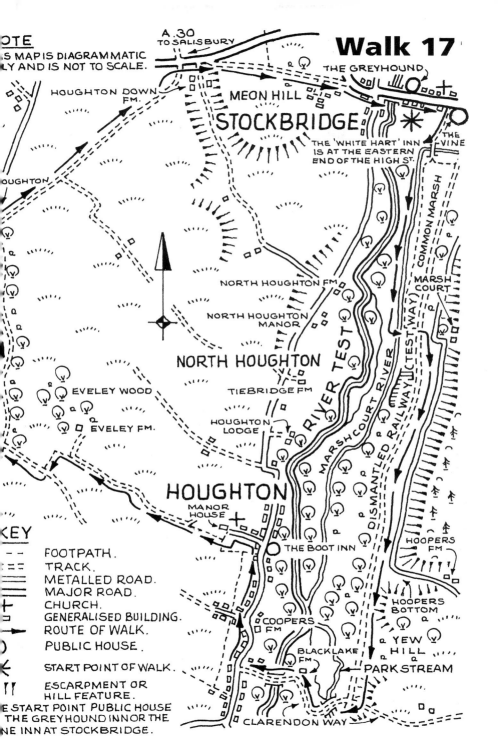

Walk 17

A.30
TO SALISBURY

THE GREYHOUND

HOUGHTON DOWN FM.

MEON HILL

STOCKBRIDGE

THE 'WHITE HART' INN
IS AT THE EASTERN
END OF THE HIGH ST.

THE VINE

OUGHTON

COMMON MARSH

NORTH HOUGHTON FM

MARSH COURT

NORTH HOUGHTON MANOR

NORTH HOUGHTON

EVELEY WOOD

TIEBRIDGE FM

EVELEY FM.

HOUGHTON LODGE

RIVER TEST

MARSHCOURT RIVER

DISMANTLED RAILWAY (TEST WAY)

HOUGHTON

MANOR HOUSE

THE BOOT INN

HOOPERS FM

HOOPERS BOTTOM

COOPERS FM

YEW HILL

BLACKLAKE FM

PARK STREAM

CLARENDON WAY

KEY

- - FOOTPATH.
== = TRACK.
≡ METALLED ROAD.
MAJOR ROAD.
✝ CHURCH.
▫ GENERALISED BUILDING.
→ ROUTE OF WALK.
◯ PUBLIC HOUSE.

⚹ START POINT OF WALK.

⌁⌁ ESCARPMENT OR
HILL FEATURE.

E START POINT PUBLIC HOUSE
THE GREYHOUND INN OR THE
NE INN AT STOCKBRIDGE.

reach the Boot Inn. On certain summer days, if time allows, it is worth venturing further along the lane to visit the beautiful riverside gardens at Houghton Lodge. Otherwise, if the pub is open, relax in their riverside garden with a refreshing drink before resuming your walk, which heads up the lane opposite the inn, waymarked to the church.

Pass the memorial cross and gently climb uphill passing some large houses before reaching All Saints church. Opposite the church lych-gate a fingerpost, close to the gates to the Manor House, directs you along a narrow path between fencing to a stile where a further sign arrows you right onto the grass verge beside the drive to the house. Your path gradually ascends, passing to the left of the properties to a stile flanking a metal gate. Maintain your uphill course out of the Test Valley, on a grassy path along the right-hand edge of a field with good views unfolding behind you down the valley and across downland beyond.

Pass beneath the electric power lines, then where the hedge you have been following terminates, keep ahead to join a stony grass-centred farm track which cuts across a vast arable field. High flying skylarks should accompany your stride as you make your way to the top of the rise, which now affords splendid views across the Wallop Brook towards Broughton Hill and Whiteshoot Hill. Peaceful downland scenes encompass you. For a moment we wished we were in the silent world of the hot-air balloon that drifted across the valley — a common sight in this area — in order to get a birds-eye view of this beautiful landscape.

With mind back on terra firma, we kept straight on where the track veers sharp right towards Eveley Farm, to follow a grassy track alongside a hedge. On reaching a field entrance and a yellow-arrowed post, turn left along a path beside another hedge to a stile in the field corner. Climb the stile to join a wide rutted grass track, turn right, then with open views gently descend to a T-junction of established tracks. Here, a conveniently placed bench provides a welcome and tranquil resting place to recoup some energy for the last stage of the walk.

Suitably refreshed, turn right along an old hedged trackway, which soon becomes beech-lined in places as you gently undulate northwards to a lane. Just before the lane turn right onto another wide and hedged green lane, a popular by-way for horse and mountain bike riders. Away to your left the wooded clumps of Danebury and Chattis Hills can be seen beyond the hustle and bustle of the A30. Eventually this track leads you downhill past Broughton Down Farm and West Lodge to what is a fast stretch of the A30. Luckily, you are not subjected to the danger of this road for long. Turn right and walk along the grass verge for a short distance to join the metalled drive entrance to Broughton Down House. Proceed ahead along the side road, parallel to the A30, passing East Lodge and gently climb uphill, the tarmac soon giving way to a stony track as it bears away from the road

Remain on this track and pass over Meon Hill, then descend through scrub to a tarmac turning area and entrance to a small housing estate and Stockbridge school. Proceed downhill towards Stockbridge High Street, soon to follow the footway beside the A30 into the village centre and your transport.

River valley and downland near Nether Wallop

WALK 18
Up to 3 ¹/₂ hours
6 miles
Walk begins page 109

Background to the Walk

The Wallops — Nether, Middle and Over — Are a string of villages linked by the little Wallop Brook, which rises from the chalk in Townsend Field, just north of Over Wallop and gently meanders its way south east-wards to join the River Test at Bossington, near Houghton. 'Wallop' simply means 'valley of the stream', but it is not just the unusual name that the villages are noted for. Nether and Over contain some of the most attractive old cottages to be found in Hampshire.

The largest of the three villages is Nether which lines the willow-edged brook for over a mile-and-a-quarter. Its maze of tiny streets are full of brick and timbered thatched cottages and is a most enchanting village to stroll around. The best view of the village and river valley is from the church which is set up on the hill.

The medieval church of St Andrew is well worth exploring for it conceals some fine treasures, the most remarkable being its collection of wall paintings, which are the finest in Hampshire. The earliest and most important is a figure of Christ in Majesty supported by flying angels which can be found above the chancel arch. It is in the style of the 11th century Winchester School of Artists and is the only known fragment of an Anglo-Saxon mural painting and is of very great inter-est to art historians. Other rare 15th century paintings can be found on the south wall of the nave. One is a warning to Sabbath-breakers depicting Christ injured by working tools, the result of working on a Sunday and another painting is of St. George slaying the Dragon, which represents the defeat of evil by the inherent goodness' of Christianity.

Maps
Landranger 1:50,000
Sheets 184 and 185
Pathfinder 1:25,000
Sheet SU23/33
Map Reference of Start/
Finish SU304364

How to get there
The Wallops lie mid-way between Salisbury and Andover on A343. From Andover take A3057 south for Stockbridge and Romsey, then join A303 and head westwards. At the next junction take A343 south for Salisbury for five-and-a-half miles to Middle Wallop, then turn left to follow the valley bottom road into Nether Wallop. The church lies on the right-hand side of the valley. If starting the walk from Over Wallop, turn right off A343 in Middle Wallop. From Salisbury follow signs M3, A30 London and Andover and head north eastwards soon to merge with A343 for Andover. In Middle Wallop turn right for Nether Wallop, left for Over Wallop. Hampshire Bus service 76/76A between Andover and Salisbury stops in Middle Wallop and occasionally diverts to Nether and Over Wallop.

Pub facilities

Five Bells, Nether Wallop

This 17th century white-painted pub was once a farmhouse and is named after the five bells in the church tower. The simple unadorned interior comprises a large through-room with wall benches, low stools, darkwood pub furniture and an open fire. There is also a small games room with a bar billiards table. The collection of helicopter photos indicate the proximity of the air base at Middle Wallop. The pub is owned by Marstons and serves their Best Bitter, Pedigree and Mild. Opening times 1100-1500 and 1800-2300 and usual Sunday hours. Bar food is good value, the menu featuring filled jacket potatoes, Wallop longboats — filled baguettes — soup and roll, ploughmans, toasted sandwiches, chicken Kiev, Cornish pasty, pizza, gammon steak and a range of daily specials. Food can be ordered between 1200-1400 and 1800-2200. Children are dogs are welcome inside. The garden boasts an excellent selection of play equipment.

White Hart, Over Wallop

(Pictured above right)
An attractive village inn with a thatched roof and porch, splendidly restored after a severe fire in recent years. A friendly welcome awaits walkers within the comfortable lounge bar, which is furnished with tapestry-covered wall benches and darkwood pub tables and chairs. There is a fine brick fireplace with a warming log fire in winter. A more sparsely furnished public bar houses the bar billiards,

Also worth finding in the church is the brass of Maria Gore (1436), the only brass portrait of a princess in the country, hidden under a mat in the nave. Dominating the churchyard is the eye-catching 15ft-high, pyramidal tomb of Francis Douce, who died in 1760.

A little further up the valley is the much sparser settlement of Middle Wallop, which has had much of its charm tempered over the years by its 20th century role as an airforce base and also by being on the busy Salisbury to Andover road. The main attraction to the visitor who has an interest in military and flying history is the Museum of Army Flying. It houses a collection of flying machines which depict the role of army flying since the late 19th century. Modern display techniques, including dioramas, tableaux, models, photographs and uniforms help bring this back to life.

Although less dense and smaller than Nether Wallop, Over Wallop has the same charm and character with an assortment of old thatched and cob cottages lining the Wallop Brook. The first mention of the village is in the Domesday Book of Hampshire in 1086, where it is described as 'other Wallope'. The village is recorded as a separate parish in 1291 and a further significant date is 1342 when a certain Richard de Wallop, who resided at the Manor, was given the patronage of St Peter's church. The patronage of the church has remained in the hands of the Wallop family ever since, the present patron being the Earl of Portsmouth. The Wallop family Manor is thought to have been either Brockhurst Cottage — a 16th century building, now consisting of three cottages — or Townsend House. Only recently the last of a long line of aristocratic Wallops actually living in the village died.

The church of St Peter which stands today overlooking a river meadow, is the result of a considerable amount of restoration during the 1860s, when a new chancel and tower were built and the rest of the building redesigned, by the architect of Truro Cathedral — J.L. Pearson. The downland surrounding the village i rich farming land and at one time the village wa totally dependant on agriculture, as the presence of a large number of farms along the main street indicates Only two working farms exist today along this street

Walk 18

Distance: *Allow three-and-a-half hours for this walk of six miles.*

pool table and darts. Flowers Original, Boddingtons Bitter and Strongs Country are dispensed on handpump between 1100-1500 and 1800-2300 and during the usual Sunday hours. A hearty selection of bar food includes good walking snacks — ploughmans, thick soups, sandwiches — plus chicken curry, ham, egg and chips, and gammon and chicken served with either chips or jacket potatoes. Food is available 1200-1400 and Thursday to Saturday 1800-2100.

Park your car near the church on the south side of the village and begin your walk by exploring the fascinating interior of St Andrew's and absorbing the delightful views that the churchyard affords over the village and valley. If the church door is locked the key can be obtained at 1, Church Road, just down the lane. Leave the churchyard and return down the lane to begin your stroll around the charming village lanes. Keep left by the bridge over Wallop Brook, to pass Old Forge Cottage and the converted chapel and follow the lane passing a selection of attractive cottages — Old Brooke Farm, Pear Tree Cottage, Jasmine Cottage, Drum Cottage — until you reach a T-junction.

If you require refreshment before your walk the Five Bells lies opposite. Otherwise, turn right and walk down the lane, passing the village shop and a few more idyllic cottages, a scene that is regularly featured in the Miss Marple series on television. Pass the Old Butchers Arms, which closed in 1972, then follow the lane round to the right and cross the bridge over the gently flowing Wallop Brook. At the main village road, turn left for a short distance, then cross over and walk up a metalled lane beside a brick wall topped with a pitched tiled roof. Beyond a black wooden barn, lookout for a fingerpost pointing you left to a metal stile, then follow a wooden fence left-handed along a narrow grassy strip of land. Wallop House is soon visible in the trees on the other side of the valley.

When you reach the end of the paddock fencing, keep straight on along the top of the field, following the predominantly yew-lined hedge to a stile in the far corner. Proceed along the hedge on a defined path to the rear of gardens to another stile, then continue over a further two arrowed stiles to a metalled lane. At certain times of the day your ramble may be interrupted by helicopters and planes, as they land and take-off from the airfield, just over the down to your right.

Cross the lane and stile beyond, then shortly cross a stile created from breeze-blocks in the left-hand corner of the field. Turn right along a narrow hedged path, your route passing behind some large gardens, crossing two more stiles before dropping down five steps onto a lane. Briefly bear right, then turn left at the waymarker post to follow the path beside a bungalow. Pass through two fence-type stiles and follow the wire fenced path left, then at the end of the fence bear right to a stile. You now bear right again to climb another stile, following the yellow arrow left behind a bungalow and fence.

Near the garage, pass through a small enclosure for animals — remembering to close the gate — to a stile in the field corner. Follow the yellow arrow to another stile, then keep to the left-hand edge of pasture, across a further stile, then maintain course alongside a wall to join a defined path beyond the next stile. Pass to the side of a bungalow and drop down onto the busy A343 Salisbury to Andover road, on the edge of Middle Wallop. Taking great care, walk across the road, go up a few stone steps into a field and follow its left-hand perimeter by a cream-painted weather-boarded house to a metal stile.

Your path now crosses a yard, two metal stiles and the small brook in between, then becomes a narrow fenced path alongside a timber yard. Climb another metal stile, then at a crossroads of tracks and Hampshire County Council sign, proceed straight on to a small wooden gate and follow the quiet tree-lined path towards Over Wallop village and church, now visible away to your left. Keep ahead when you reach a wide farm track, then on merging with a metalled lane continue straight on, soon to reach a T-junction. Turn left down King Lane, passing attractive cottages as you descend to the memorial cross and the village centre.

If you wish to visit St Peter's church cross over by the thatched barn and follow the path up to the much restored flint church, which overlooks the river meadow. The main street is lined with some fine examples of typical Hampshire thatched cottages, many of them constructed with chalk cob, half-timber with either wattle and daub or brick infilling, set on flint foundations. Originally they were simple farm workers cottages, many of them more than one dwelling, until the 1960s when affluent retired folk and commuters began to improve and convert them.

From the memorial cross follow the village street right to where Salisbury Lane bears off left across Wallop Brook. If you are thirsty, a parched throat can be refreshed at the thatched White Hart Inn, which is located a little further up the main street on your right. Venture further and you will come to the imposing Georgian-style Townsend Manor, once the Dower House of the 5th Countess of Portsmouth and opposite, behind a fine thatched cob wall is a delightful garden.

Your route heads south up Salisbury Lane past the magnificent 16th century thatched Brockhurst Cottages, once the residence of the Wallop family, following

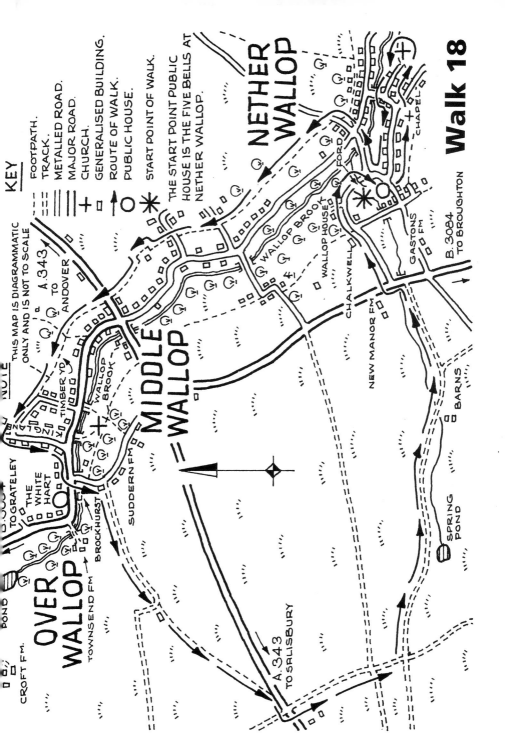

Walk 18

KEY

- – – – FOOTPATH.
- ═ ═ ═ TRACK.
- ═══ METALLED ROAD.
- ═╪═ MAJOR ROAD.
- ✝ CHURCH.
- ▢ GENERALISED BUILDING.
- ⟶ ROUTE OF WALK.
- ○ PUBLIC HOUSE.
- ✳ START POINT OF WALK.

THE START POINT PUBLIC HOUSE IS THE FIVE BELLS AT NETHER WALLOP.

NOTE
THIS MAP IS DIAGRAMMATIC ONLY AND IS NOT TO SCALE

NETHER WALLOP

CHAPEL

FORD

WALLOP BROOK

WALLOP HOUSE

CHALKWELL

GASTONS FM.

B.3084 TO BROUGHTON

A.343 TO ANDOVER

TIMBER YD.

WALLOP BROOK

MIDDLE WALLOP

SUDDERN FM.

NEW MANOR FM.

BARNS

SPRING POND

A.343 TO SALISBURY

OVER WALLOP

CROFT FM.

POND

TO GRATELEY

THE WHITE HART

TOWNSEND FM.

BROCKHURST

the lane round a left-hand bend to a white cottage, called Hope Cottage. Turn right onto the established grass centred track — Old Salisbury Lane — before the cottage, then keep left at an old round corrugated barn to follow a grass track along the line of telegraph poles. For the first time on the walk you are out of the valley and striding across open fertile downland, with good views all round.

When you reach the fast and busy main road (A343) cross over onto the wide grassy verge and follow it south westwards for about 100 yards to a stony earth track on your left. Leave the main road, then keep left where the track forks and join a wide hedged grass thoroughfare, this time with superb rolling downland scenes towards the chalk scarp slope of Broughton Down. At the first crossroads of green lanes, proceed straight on, then in a short distance at the next junction of by-ways, turn left to follow another fine hedged track in a south easterly direction through farmland. This track can be muddy, especially when you arrive at the spring pond, which lies in the field to your right. The crystal clear water that emerges from the pond runs down a channel alongside your path.

Shortly, pass a gate and track leading to a barn, then where the track veers sharp right, bear off left along a defined grassy path, parallel to the stream. The path becomes hedged and brings you to the B3084 where you turn left for a little way, before turning right onto a narrow metalled lane towards Nether Wallop. At a grassy area with four silver birch trees, bear left past the driveway to Chalkwell and follow the lane downhill passing the entrance to Wallop House, then cross the small footbridge beside the ford and bear right to rejoin your outward route back into the village centre for the Five Bells and the church.

Till & Wylye Valley footpaths from Berwick St. James

WALK 19
Up to 4 hours
6 ½ miles
Walk begins page 115

Background to the Walk

Unlike many of the chalk downland valleys across the Salisbury Plain, the valley of the River Till is the only one with a permanent flow of water. Numerous springs high up in the heart of the Plain continuously feed the little river, which rises near Tilshead and flows south through Shrewton, Winterbourne Stoke and Berwick St. James before merging with the much larger River Wylye at Stapleford.

Under normal conditions, even in the wettest of winters, the porous nature of chalk will absorb the rainfall, but occasionally under quite exceptional conditions flash floods can occur across chalk downland. A particularly devastating flood, created by a rapid thaw of snow, swept off the Plain into the Till Valley in January 1841 and wrought havoc through the villages of Tilshead, Orcheston, Shrewton and Winterbourne Stoke, destroying 47 houses and numerous farms. In Tilshead today, the river is piped under the village in order to avert the danger of another flood.

Our walk explores the delightfully unspoilt lower reaches of the River Till, where the tiny river valley widens and merges with the more swiftly flowing River Wylye as it progresses south to Wilton, Salisbury and the River Avon.

Berwick St. James nestles beside the river and is compactly arranged in linear fashion along the B3083. 'Berwick' means an outlying grange or farm, with the saintly part of the village name originating from the dedication of the fine Norman-built church that lies beside the main village road. Constructed of flint and stone it has a central tower with round headed win-

Maps
Landranger 1:50,000
Sheet 185
Pathfinder 1:25,000
Sheet SU 03/13
Map reference of Start/
Finish SU072395

How to get there
Berwick St James nestles in the Till valley approximately a mile north of the A36 at Stapleford and eight-and-a-half miles north west of Salisbury. From Salisbury town centre follow signs for 'the West, A30, A303' towards Wilton and Warminster on A36. At the roundabout in Wilton go straight across, remaining on A36 through South Newton and Stoford to Stapleford. Turn right onto B3083 and pass through Stapleford village for Berwick St James. The Boot is located at the far end of the village. From Andover take A3057 Stockbridge/Romsey road south, then join A303 and head west leaving it at the first junction to follow A343 for Salisbury. Merge with A30 and proceed into Salisbury. At the first main roundabout take the fourth exit and follow signs for Warminster and the West. Wilts and Dorset service 2 between Salisbury and Devizes, via Wilton stops

Right: Boot Inn, Berwick St, James

at Stoford and opposite the Boot in Berwick St James. Wilts and Dorset/Hampshire Bus services 7, 8 and 9, Hampshire Bus service 76/ 76A and fast and frequent trains link Salisbury to Andover.

Pub facilities
Boot Inn, Berwick St James
An attractive stone and flint village local with a traditional unspoilt interior and a well tended garden with colourful flower borders and various benches. The cosy lounge bar has a huge inglenook and the homely public bar a lovely old woodblock floor and stone mullioned windows. The pub once provided emergency shoe/ boot repairs for weary travellers trekking west along the old road. Today it is known locally for its pumpkin championships — UK champions 1991 — and for its thriving Gardening Club. The bar opens between 1200-1400 (1500 Saturday and Sundays) and 1900-2300, but the pub is closed on Monday lunchtimes. Food is available by prior arrangement and at lunchtimes only, but Sunday walkers can enjoy the regular summer lunchtime barbecue feast. Excellent Wadworth IPA and 6X are dispensed by handpump. Dogs are welcome inside as are children if the weather is inclement. Walkers are welcome to park at the pub, if permission is asked.

dows, a Perpendicular porch and a notable Norman doorway with zig-zag mouldings. Inside is a splendid 13th century arch which spans the width of the chancel and a Norman font. Unfortunately for us a remarkable 13th century chalice that once belonged to the church is now exhibited in the British Museum.

A little further down the valley, at the point where the two rivers converge, is the delightful village of Stapleford with green banks, thatched cottages clustering about the way to the church. There are seven other Staplefords in England, for Stapleford is the name given by the Saxons to a common feature of 'a ford marked by a post or staple' which would probably serve to indicate the shallowest place in the stream. In Wiltshire it became the name of a strategic point where the road from Old Sarum to Bath crosses the Till. It was an important line of communication and it is still marked on the map as 'Herepath'. This is the road on which Alfred's Saxon army probably marched along to defeat the Danes and may have possibly been used by Roman legionnaires. We can surmise this from the prescence on Stapleford Down of an earthwork known as South Kite, which is thought to have been the site of a Roman Camp.

There are four distinct parts to the village. Uppington lies a mile north of the ford and is represented by two houses, while in between is the hamlet known as Church Street named after St. Mary's church. On the right bank of the stream is 'the settlement opposite' or

Left: Stapleford and the church

Pelican Inn, Stapleford
Popular roadside inn with an attractive garden with play area fronting the River Till and busy with a good food trade. Named after one of the ships in the Armada fleet, it is an old coaching inn which has been tastefully extended, the old stables now housing the restaurant area. Doors open from 1100-1430 (1500 Saturday) and 1800-2300 for liquid refreshment which includes a range of four regularly changing real ales, such as King Alfred Pendragon, Ringwood Best and Old Thumper and Otter Ale, plus a good scrumpy cider from Inch's. A blackboard menu highlights the daily specials which may include chicken and mushroom pie, cheese lattice flan, quiches and a freshly prepared soup, cream of Stilton for example. The regular menu ranges from hearty light snacks — filled rolls, sandwiches and ploughmans — and salads to steak and kidney pie, lasagne, chicken Kiev, steaks, grills and vegetarian options like lentil and nut casserole. Food is available 1200-1400 (1430 Saturday) and 1800-2130. Children are welcolme in the restaurant area but dogs are not allowed in the building. Walkers must ask permission if planning to leave their vehicles in the car park.

Overstreet, which lies clustered beside a castle mound, it has not as yet been excavated but probably dates from the 12th century. Finally, Serrington — 'the farm by the water' — which is better known as Southington and comprises the Pelican Inn and a few other dwellings beside the A36. The Till, previously crossed via a ford, was bridged here some 350 years ago.

St. Mary's church was built of flint and stone over 800 years ago, but most of what we see dates from the 14th century. However, the doorway, its richly decorated arch and the simple bowl of the font immediately inside belong to the late 12th century, as do the four arches of the nave resting on a series of massive drum columns, decorated by alternating bands of Chilmark stone and green sandstone.

Walk 19

Distance: *Up to four hours for this walk of six-and-a-half miles.*

The Boot public house at the northern edge of the village is a friendly and unspoilt local and a good starting point for this country ramble. However I must point out that bar food is only available by prior arrangement, so those walkers seeking refreshment should either contact the pub first, plan to eat at the Pelican Inn in Stapleford or the Swan Inn at Stoford, or begin the walk from one of these hostelries.

From the Boot head south along the footway beside the B3083 and walk the length of the village, passing St.

Right: The Avon Valley

Swan Inn, Stoford
Set hard beside the A36, the Swan is a favourite halt for travellers due to its fine riverside garden and the extensive range of food on offer. Two real ales are generally available — Morland Old Speckled Hen, Wadworth 6X and a large blackboard lists the dishes on offer, which have included chilli, pork and cider casserole, cottage pie, lasagne, spaghetti Bolognaise, steaks, beef and kidney suet pudding and duck a la orange. Various salads and snacks like sandwiches, generously filled rolls and ploughmans are always featured. Food is served 1200-1400 and 1830-2130, with liquid refreshment available between 1100-1430 and 1800-2300 with the usual Sunday hours. Children are welcome inside and can choose from their own menu. Overnight accommodation.

James's church and an assortment of attractive cottages until you reach the sharp left-hand bend and bridge over the River Till. Bear off right with the fingerpost waymarker to join a grass-centred track alongside the peaceful, idly flowing stream. On reaching the end of this defined track, keep right away from the stream to follow an established path uphill and beside the left-hand hedge of an open arable field. At the crest of this short undemanding climb, you will be rewarded with serene rural views across the lush Till valley and south over rolling arable downland towards Grovely Wood, topping the horizon beyond the Wyly valley.

Soon you will pass through a small wooden swing gate, your path beyond following a defined break between crop fields towards a farm complex nestling in the trees ahead. In a little way merge with a stony track, keep straight on where it veers left to the group of farm buildings, then pass between two barns to join the main concrete farm road. Turn left, gently descend into the valley bottom, passing Manor Farm and Castle Cottage. All that exists of Stapleford Castle, a 12th century earthwork, is a tree-covered mound away to your left. Shortly, you will reach the narrow valley lane with the tiny hamlet of Over Street, one of the four settlements comprising Stapleford village, spreading southwards.

Bear left to follow the lane towards the heart of the village — Church Street – crossing sheep-grazed meadowland and then the Till via Bury Bridge. If time permits, go through the small gate on your left into a delightful grassy area, where a riverside bench makes an ideal spot for a few moments rest. The river at this point

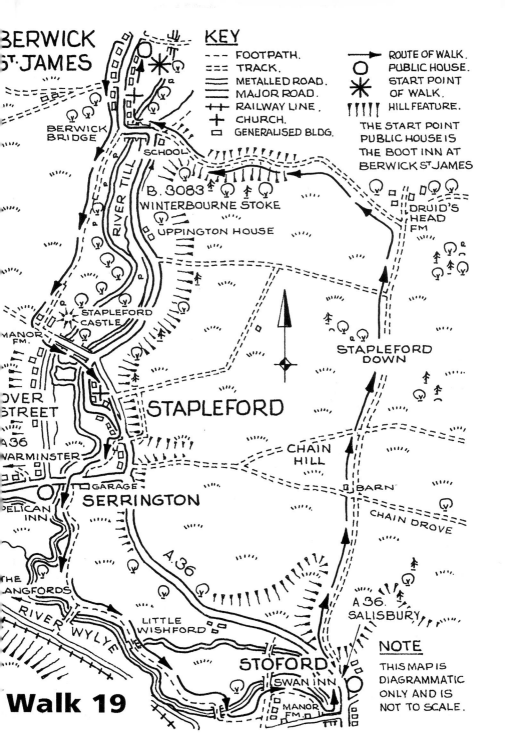

BERWICK
ST JAMES

KEY

- - - FOOTPATH.
=== TRACK.
≡ METALLED ROAD.
≡ MAJOR ROAD.
+—+ RAILWAY LINE.
+ CHURCH.
☐ GENERALISED BLDG.

→ ROUTE OF WALK.
◯ PUBLIC HOUSE.
✳ START POINT
OF WALK.
🙰🙰🙰🙰🙰 HILL FEATURE.

THE START POINT
PUBLIC HOUSE IS
THE BOOT INN AT
BERWICK ST JAMES

BERWICK
BRIDGE

SCHOOL

RIVER TILL

B.3083
WINTERBOURNE STOKE

UPPINGTON HOUSE

DRUID'S
HEAD
FM.

STAPLEFORD
CASTLE

MANOR
FM.

STAPLEFORD
DOWN

OVER
STREET

A36
WARMINSTER

STAPLEFORD

CHAIN
HILL

GARAGE

SERRINGTON

BARN

CHAIN DROVE

PELICAN
INN

A.36

THE
LANGFORDS

RIVER WYLYE

LITTLE
WISHFORD

A.36
SALISBURY

NOTE

THIS MAP IS
DIAGRAMMATIC
ONLY AND IS
NOT TO SCALE.

STOFORD

SWAN INN

MANOR
FM.

Walk 19

is overhung by sallow and fringed with willow and is haven to duck, moorhen and if you are lucky you may see kingfisher and heron. At the crossroads of lanes, go straight over the B-road and head uphill to follow a quiet lane that leads you round the back of the village. Shortly, you will drop down to rejoin the busier main village street. The attractive row of whitewashed cottages and St. Mary's church — an idyllic village scene — are well worth closer inspection by turning right along the narrow footway.

The main route crosses the B3083 onto a pitted tarmac track that passes between garages, before becoming a grass-centred track as it bears left in front of Seymour Cottage. Keep right with the wall to join a narrow tarmac path that traverses the lush meadowland of the Till valley to the A36 and the group of dwellings known as Serrington. Pass through a small wooden gate opposite the Shell garage and turn right along the footpath to the Pelican Bridge. Cross the Till if you require refreshment at the Pelican Inn, otherwise cross the fast and busy main road to climb a stile flanking a metal gate.

Follow the grassy path between the river bank and fence to a further stile located beside a 'Private fishing' sign. Beyond the stile, bear half-right along a defined meadow path, parallel with the river, cross a stile and tiny plank bridge, then wend your way along a narrow earth path to a wooden footbridge and enter a large riverside meadow. At this point you are very close to the confluence of the Till and Wylye and the worn grass path bears diagonally left across the open valley pasture to the banks of the Wylye and a sluice gate. This is a splendid spot and one that can be enjoyed by all and not just reserved for the pleasures of fee-paying fishermen. We walked this way on a warm June afternoon and the willow-fringed riverbank, cattle-filled meadows and surrounding fertile downland painted a most tranquil summer country scene.

Do not cross the plank bridge over the sluice gate, instead head south along the riverbank, following the established path. Groups of swans can often be seen feeding and gliding effortlessly through the crystal clear water. When you reach the point where the river meanders to the right away from you, keep left of the old gate posts to follow the right-hand edge of pasture to a stile in the field corner. Almost immediately climb another stile, then head straight across pasture to rejoin the reed-fringed riverbank. With enjoyable valley scenes at every glance proceed along the right-hand edge of pasture, passing a metal gate and river bridge, then in a short distance on nearing the perimeter of the meadow, bear off left through grass beside the river to a stile. Climb the stile, then negotiate two footbridges over a small tributary stream, a further stile before resuming your riverside stroll.

On reaching a wooden footbridge spanning the river, proceed ahead on a worn path that cuts across a meander and heads towards an attractive thatched cottage on the far bank of the river. Rejoin the Wylye river, which at this point is a good spot to watch fishermen practising the art of fly-fishing for trout and continue along the riverbank to a wooden footbridge over the river. Cross the Wylye, turn left along its bank looking out for some of the flycatchers, wagtails, wrens and moorhen that enjoy this habitat, then in 100 yards or so gradually bear right away from the river towards Manor Farm and a stile which is visible in paddock fencing.

Beyond the stile, turn left through a pair of wooden gates to join a gravel track, then on arriving at a footpath fingerpost waymarking a route back across the river to Little Wishford, turn right through a metal gate beside it. Go across a small paddock and through a further gate, then keep right-handed through a series of sheep-grazed meadows along the valley bottom with the village of Great Wishford coming into view away to your right. Eventually climb a stile onto a metalled lane, turn right if you have the time and or the desire to explore Great Wishford (see Walk 15), otherwise turn left to cross Stoford Bridge and reach the A36.

Turn left along the footway and shortly enter the car park of the Swan Inn. The delightful riverside garden is a super place in which to relax with a pint and to admire the view across the meadows to Great Wishford. Walk to the far end of the car park, carefully cross the A36 to join a wide tree-lined, grass-centred track that begins to ascend the valley. Emerge from the trees and continue your gentle climb to the top of Chain Hill, regularly pausing to take in the magnificent vistas that unfold all around you — you can, at intervals, see across the valley and Great Wishford to Grovely Wood, west along the broad valley towards Warminster and soon north and eastwards to far-distant horizons of Marlborough and the North Hampshire Downs.

Maintain your course along this wide thoroughfare, across two crossroads of by-ways, then traverse Stapleford Down to Druids Head Farm. Turn left just before the farm complex and descends a stony track that wends its way down a dry valley back into the Till valley and Berwick St. James. This established green way was part of the Harrow Way or Shrine Way, an ancient route that linked Dover in Kent to Somerset and Dorset by way of Canterbury, North Downs, Stonehenge and Grovely Ridge. When you reach the valley road by the now redundant village school, cross the Till and retrace your steps back through the village to the Boot.

Exploring the Avon Valley & Old Sarum from Salisbury

Maps
Landranger 1:50,000
Sheet 185
Pathfinder 1:25,000
Sheet SU 03/13
Map reference of Start/
Finish SU142303

How to get there
The main city centre car park is well signposted and can be accessed from Castle Street, from Fisherton Street near the railway station and easily from the A36 ring-road. The Haunch of Venison is located opposite the Poultry Cross in the heart of the town and can be reached from the car park by walking through the small shopping area beyond Sainsbury's, crossing the Avon and passing through the covered walkway beside the library to emerge opposite the Market Square. Turn right into Minster Street and keep to the right-hand side for the pub. Salisbury can be reached from Andover by taking A3057 Stockbridge/Romsey road from the town centre, then heading west along A303 for a mile to link with A343 for Salisbury. Merge with A30 and enter Salisbury, then at the first major roundabout take the fourth exit 'The West, Warminster A36' to join the ring-road. Keep straight on over the next roundabout and

Background to the Walk

Salisbury, or New Sarum, built at the confluence of four rivers and sheltered by downland, is one of the most beautiful cathedral cities in Britain. Relatively free from sprawling suburbs and high-rise developments common in most cities, the surrounding countryside comes in to meet the city streets along the r iver valleys. The skyline is dominated by the majestic spire of the cathedral, which makes a graceful centrepiece to the unified city and is now restored to its former glory since the scaffolding, which seemed to have been there for years has been removed. Throughout the centre, buildings of all styles blend harmoniously — from medieval gabled houses, historic inns and market places to stately pedimented Georgian houses and even the modern shopping centre.

Salisbury was founded in 1220 following the abandonment of the Norman cathedral built on the fortified hill of Old Sarum. Bishop Richard Poore completed the new cathedral in the remarkably short time of 38 years and as a result it is built largely in a single style — Early English Gothic — unlike many other medieval English cathedrals. The tower and spire, with a combined height of 404 ft. — the tallest in England — were added in 1334 and the west front of the building is most lavishly decorated. It has row upon row of statues in niches.

The rich and spacious interior contains huge graceful columns of Purbeck stone, which line the high-vaulted nave and many windows add to the airy, dignified interior. There are numerous impressive tombs and effigies in the nave, the oldest being that of

William Longespée, Earl of Salisbury who was buried here in 1226. He was a witness to the signing of the Magna Carta in 1215 by King John and one of the four surviving originals of this document is on display in the Chapter House. This most beautiful octagonal room is decorated with 60 scenes from the Old Testament involving about 200 carved figures. Also of note in the Cathedral is a clock dating from 1386 and claimed to be the oldest clock in the world. It has no dial but simply chimes the hours.

The Close surrounding the cathedral is the largest and finest in Britain, entered by a series of medieval gateways and containing a rich variety of architectural styles, from the 13th century to

shortly bear off left following the car park signs. Wilts and Dorset/ Hampshire Bus services 7, 8, and 9, Hampshire Bus service 76/76A and frequent trains link Salisbury with Andover.

Pub facilities
Haunch of Venison
14 Minster Street, Salisbury
(Pictured left)
Antiquity and charm ooze from this small city centre pub, which dates from 1320 when it was built as a church house for nearby St. Thomas's church. Three unspoilt rooms are generally filled with locals, businessmen and tourists enjoying the chatty music and game-free atmosphere. The rooms are affectionately known as the 'horsebox', a tiny snug bar off the entrance lobby, the 'House of Commons', the main bar with a black and white chequered stone floor, oak panelled walls, heavy beams and a large inglenook fireplace with a gleaming copper hood. Up a few steps is the 'House of Lords' a cosy upper room with small paned windows overlooking the main bar. It boasts antique leather upholstered settles, a carved oak chair and a 600-year-old fireplace with a small side window displaying a smoke-preserved mummified hand holding a pack of 18th century playing cards, which was discovered here in 1903. The pub opens from 1100-2300, the tiny pewter-topped bar dispensing Ringwood Best Bitter, Courage Best and Directors and a collection of over 100 whiskies. A rare set of antique taps for gravity fed spirits is displayed on the bar. A simple selection of good value bar snacks are available, such as vegetable soup, stuffed peppers, shepherds pie, curry, a range of filled jacket potatoes, savoury pancakes and a good choice of sandwiches and plou ghmans. Food is served 1200-1430 and 1900-2130. Upstairs the 'old english chop house' restaurant is open between 1900-2200. Children are welcome in the top bar.

the present day. Notable houses are the King's House, now exhibiting finds from Stonehenge, Old Sarum, a roman mosaic pavement and a collection of English pottery, china and glass, (open daily); Mompesson House (National Trust), a perfect example of Queen Anne architecture displaying notable plasterwork, an elegant carved oak staircase and fine period furniture, (open April to October); Malmesbury House, originally a 13th century canonry and later the home of the Earls of Malmesbury. The Orangery was used as a shelter during the Civil War and King Charles II and the composer Handel stayed in the house, (open early-April to early-October, Tuesdays to Thursdays and on Bank Holidays). Lastly, the Wardrobe, a medieval house containing the museum of the Duke of Edinburgh's Royal Regiment (open daily).

Beyond The Close, Salisbury is a delightful place to explore on foot, through a fascinating network of medieval streets and alleys lined with half-timbered and jettied houses, such as the 15th century House of John a'Port in Queen Street, the 16th century Joiners Hall in St. Ann Street and the 14th century inn, the Rose and Crown. Also worth seeking out are the hexagonally buttressed 15th century Poultry Cross, the last of four market crosses in the city, St. Thomas's church (1238) which has magnificent 15th century arcades and one of the most notable Doom paintings in England. A riverside stroll to Harnham Bridge will reveal the famous view across the Avon to the cathedral, much admired by many an artist, in particular Constable.

From New Sarum our walk not only enjoys the unspoilt beauty of the Avon Valley, but allows the opportunity to complete the historical picture of Salisbury by exploring the massive ramparts and earthworks of the original settlement of Old Sarum, set on a bleak hill overlooking the present city. Once a huge Iron Age hillfort, it was later inhabited by the Romans, Saxons, Danes and finally by the Normans who built the castle, cathedral and bishop's palace. All that remains of these are the stone foundations, much of the rest of the stone being used to build the present cathedral in the 13th century.

Old Sarum was also the place where William the Conqueror inspected his

ictorious army in 1070
nd it was once a very
rand city indeed, bus-
ling with people. To-
ay, one can roam
cross the 56 acres of
amparts and ruins
vhich are owned by
.nglish Heritage but an
dmission fee is charged
ɔ view the inner bailey
uins. The site com-
nands splendid views
ver Salisbury, the
\von Valley and far-
eaching views across
alisbury Plain and
he neighbouring
ownland.

Old Forge Cottage at Stratford-sub-Castle

Walk 20

Distance : *At least three hours for this five mile walk,
longer if you plan to linger at Old Sarum.*

here are plenty of car parks around the city centre, but by far the most convenient
or this walk and the cheapest (around 80p per day) is the main central parking
rea located behind the library and close to Tesco's and Sainsbury's. Pubs and old
oaching inns also abound. My choice of the Haunch of Venison in Minster Street
5 due to its antiquity as a building — one of the oldest in the city — and for its
enuine, unspoilt charm and character as a pub.

With the knowledge that your vehicle is safe in the car park, join the well-
narked 'Riverside Walk' which begins by the covered walkway at the back of the
brary, a short stroll from your car. Follow the river, pass round the back of the
oathouse Inn and rejoin the riverside path after crossing the entrance road to the
ar park. A word of caution is needed here as the path is also a cycle track, so be
repared to dodge wayward bikes.

This delightful path passes beneath two bridges, cleverly avoiding the hustle
nd bustle of daily town life and hugs the River Avon as you gradually emerge out
ito unspoilt countryside. Cross a road, then follow a tarmac path beside a large
reen, towards the Sports Centre situated on the other side of the river. Disregard
he small footbridge that leads to the Centre and continue to cross a bridge over
small tributary stream, then turn right onto the raised grass bank beside the main
hannel of the Avon.

Where the path narrows and proceeds beside the river through a lightly
/ooded and reedy area, bear off left away from the river across the grass to join
n established path beside a series of allotments. At the end of the chain-link fence
ɔ the allotments, bear left with the main path, which becomes tree-lined as you

Above: Walking towards Old Sarum

progress up-valley with cameo river valley views across to Old Sarum, dominating the scene away to your right. Eventually, you will reach a pitted tarmac path, turn right and shortly cross a modern bridge over the Avon. An idyllically sited mill can be spotted through the trees to your left as your path bears left through a 'walk-through' stile to merge with Mill Lane. Keep right, following the track past a few houses a garage and a cream painted cottage to the main village road in Stratford sub-Castle.

Turn right along the foot way passing some of the 17th and 18th century houses that characterise this village, then just beyond Old Forge Cottage cross the road to join a wide track waymarked beside a thatched cottage to 'Old Sarum ¹/₂ m'. This grass centred, fenced green lane gradually climbs towards the base of the ancient hillfort. Shortly, ignore a stile leading into pasture and bear sharp left with the now hedge-lined track, which leads you along the base of the fortifications.

When you reach a rough tarmac by-way, turn right uphill and soon keep right to join an unclassified lane which affords good views up the lush Avon Valley. Gently ascend passing a house with the wooded earth ramparts of Old Sarum behind and eventually reach a point where an established green way crosses the lane. Far-reaching views across the Plain and surrounding downland can be appreciated from this lofty position.

Your route now heads right across the stile flanking a gate, then along the track parallel with the outer ramparts of the hillfort to where it joins the main entrance road. Turn right and if you wish to tour the earth fortifications and deep ditches kissing gates allow free access onto the outer ramparts. To visit the inner bailey

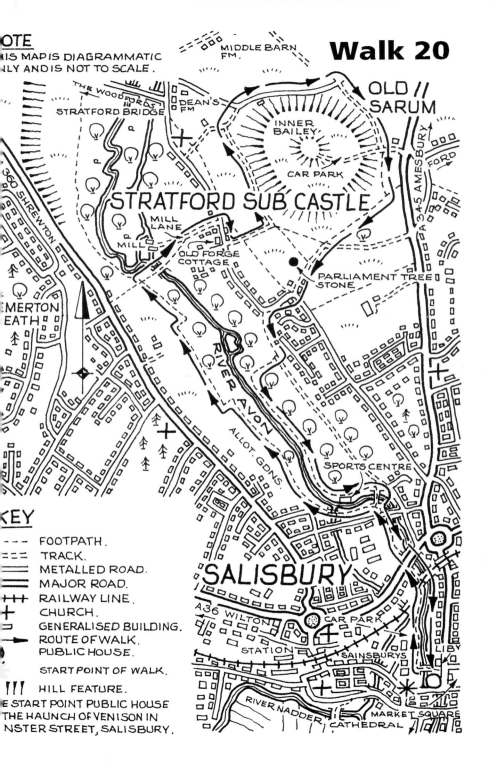

Walk 20

MIDDLE BARN FM.

OLD // SARUM

THE WOODFORD STRATFORD BRIDGE

DEAN'S FM.

INNER BAILEY

CAR PARK

360 SHREWTON

STRATFORD SUB CASTLE

MILL LANE

MILL

OLD FORGE COTTAGE

PARLIAMENT TREE STONE

MERTON EATH

RIVER AVON

ALLOT. GDNS.

SPORTS CENTRE

A 3 4 5 AMESBURY

FORD

KEY

- - - FOOTPATH.
= = = TRACK.
===== METALLED ROAD.
===== MAJOR ROAD.
+++ RAILWAY LINE.
+ CHURCH.
⊐ GENERALISED BUILDING.
➤ ROUTE OF WALK.
PUBLIC HOUSE.

START POINT OF WALK.

!!! HILL FEATURE.

E START POINT PUBLIC HOUSE
THE HAUNCH OF VENISON IN
NSTER STREET, SALISBURY.

SALISBURY

A36 WILTON

STATION

CAR PARK

SAINSBURYS

LIBY

RIVER NADDER

CATHEDRAL

MARKET SQUARE

continue along the metalled access road to the English Heritage admission hut
Time spent surveying this fascinating site will be well rewarded.

Retrace your steps through the outer earthwork and turn right through a small
gate, located beside a larger five-bar gate, to follow the path downhill off the
hillfort. Go through a further gate to where a green footpath fingerpost directs you
right away from the main road, back towards Stratford-sub-Castle.

Proceed downhill along a worn grassy path beside a fence, then as it bears right
to a stile and fingerpost, keep ahead through the hedgerow to join an old pitted
tarmac trackway — the ancient Roman Portway. Five major Roman roads meet at
Old Sarum: one from Cunetio near Marlborough, from Winchester, the Portway
from Silchester, Ackling Dyke and the main route west, emphasising how important this site was in times past.

Maintain your downhill course and shortly pass the site of the Parliament Tree
which is marked by a commemoration stone erected in 1931. Old Sarum was one
of the 'rotten boroughs' abolished by the Reform Act of 1832, when only ten voters
returned two MP's; one was the famous representative, William Pitt the Elder, the
18th century Prime Minister. They were elected whilst standing underneath the
tree which was cut down in 1905 and later replaced by the huge stone and plaque.
Continue down to the village road and keep straight on along the footway to
where the road bears sharp right.

Your route now crosses the road to where a waymarker arrows you along a path
towards the 'city centre'. With dwellings to your left and open river meadow on
your right, remain on the path where it becomes a wide stony track, then bear right
over a small plank bridge over a ditch to join a good gravel path. You are now in
the grounds of the Sports Centre. Proceed ahead, the path soon bearing left to
follow the course of the Avon before passing in front of the Centre itself. In a little
way cross a wooden footbridge over the river and turn left to retrace your outward
route back into the city centre and your transport.

· BIBLIOGRAPHY ·

Hampshire Customs, Curiosities & Country Lore — John Mann, Ensign Publications

Hampshire, The Complete Guide — Jo Draper, Dovecote Press

Hampshire and the Isle of Wight — Ed. Arthur Mee, Hodder & Stoughton

Hidden Hampshire — John Barton, Countryside Books

Illustrated Portrait of Wiltshire — Pamela Street, Robert Hale

It Happened in Hampshire — Hampshire Women's Institutes

New Hampshire Village Book — Hampshire Women's Institutes

Picture of Salisbury — Brian Green and Barry Shurlock, Ensign Publications

Pub Walks around Southampton — Peter Carne, Ensign Publications

Pub Walks in and around the New Forest — Peter Carne, Ensign Publications

Shell Book of English Villages — Ed. John Hatfield, Michael Joseph

Test Way and Clarendon Way — Barry Shurlock, HCC

Twenty Wessex Walks: Exploring Prehistoric Paths — Jane Whittle, Hobnob Press

Visitors Guide to Hampshire & the Isle of Wight — John Barton, Moorland

Wessex Leisure Guide — AA/Ordnance Survey

Wiltshire, The King's England — Ed. Arthur Mee, Hodder & Stoughton

Wiltshire — Ralph Whitlock, B T Batsford

Wiltshire Village Book — Michael Marshman, Countryside Books

Wiltshire Villages — Margaret Wilson, Ex Libris Press

Wiltshire Villages — Brian Woodruffe, Robert Hale

· ACKNOWLEDGMENTS ·

In compiling this new collection of walks, I would like to acknowledge th
important contribution that my friend and colleague Bonita Toms has made
this, my second volume in the Pub Walks series. Bonita accompanied me on all th
walks, making invaluable observations and notes along the way and taking th
photographs which appear with the text. I am most grateful for her enthusiasr
support and companionship throughout this project.

I would like to thank Jack Street for his exemplary, detailed sketch maps th
accompany each walk description. They are a vital element in each walk, hig
lighting the landmarks and buildings mentioned in the text and instilling con
dence in novice walkers.

I am also grateful to the landlords of the featured pubs, for their cooperation ar
the enthusiasm they expressed in the concept of Pub Walks. I must thank th
numerous individuals who have helped by contributing background informatic
and those that have answered queries on bus timetables, opening times and righ
of way.

· The PUB WALKS Series ·

Pub Walks on the Isle of Wight
Pub Walks around the New Forest
Pub Walks in and around the New Forest
Pub Walks around Portsmouth and the South Downs
Pub Walks around Southampton and Central Hampshire
Pub Walks around Camberley and the North Hampshire Downs
Pub Walks around Farnham and the Western Weald
Pub Walks around Winchester and North Hampshire
Pub Walks around Basingstoke and Central Hampshire
Pub Walks around Bristol and the Avon Valley
Pub Walks around Bath and the Avon Valley
Pub Walks around Oxford and the Thames Valley
Pub Walks around Chester and Wrexham
Pub Walks around Stratford-upon-Avon and Worcester
Pub Walks around Newcastle and the Tyne Valley
Pub Walks around Gloucester and Cheltenham

If you would like to contribute to this series please submit a complete sample chapter from
your chosen area and send it to: Ensign Publications, 2 Redcar Street, Southampton SO1 5LL